Acknowledgements

Thanks to my dear mentors, Alice, Marc, Dan, Genet, Jeff, Stephen, who contributed with feedback and enthusiasm. Your friendship and guidance are blessings that have added and continue to add meaning to my growth.

To my mother, Zübeyde, whose courage and capacity have inspired and strengthened my enthusiasm for life,

My father, Osman Nidai, whose wisdom and generous heart has calmed my spirit,

My brother, Ali Rayet, whose child-like spirit has gemmed our shared journeys.

"Let yourself be silently drawn by the strange pull of what you really love.

It will not lead you astray"

-Rumi

On the Page	Size of Painting (inches)	Page #

The Artists Note

Theme's

Derya's paintings are abstract expressions of singular moments. While she paints in bold and cathartic expressions, she is equally compelled painting soft, nostalgic, and mysterious effects. Derya's pieces focus the audience on a journey that explores emotions of love, joy, sadness, and grief and longing.

Art Titles

Due to her multi-lingual background, Derya's conceptualization of a moment is strongly influenced by her verbal reasoning and linguistic expressions. For example, while in the English language there is one word for "beautiful", in Turkish there are six variants. Because these variants do not have exact English translations, Derya uses the Turkish variant in the title and describes the piece in English through her poetry. This introduction invites the perceiver to explore familiar emotions using unfamiliar linguistic reasoning.

Style

Derya uses geometrism and impressionism to invite an exploration of space. As rigid structures from geometrism expand and contract the perception of space, impressionistic soft colors and blended brush strokes evoke movement and stillness within this space. The viewer is then drawn into an exploration of time influenced and highlighted by the experience of surroundings, color, movement and stillness.

Color

Derya's use of metallic hues among soft tones creates a contradiction of color and style. As these effects highlight accents within an area, the viewer is invited to a psychic exploration that reflects on boundaries of thought and emotion within the same space.

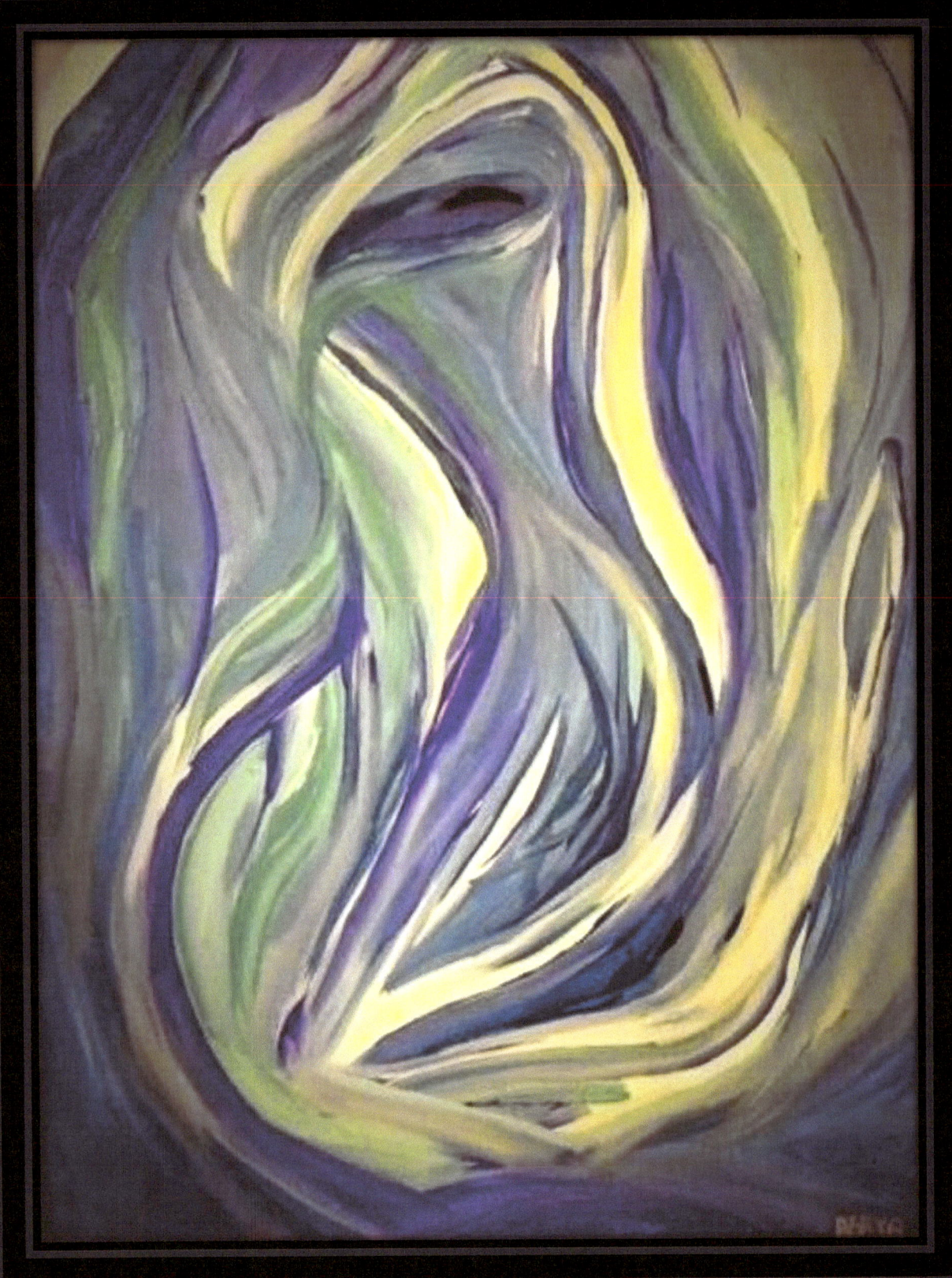

Vessel

What flows within and out. Fills and empties. Simultaneously.
Building, destroying and renewing.
All that which was known.
All that which is thought knowing

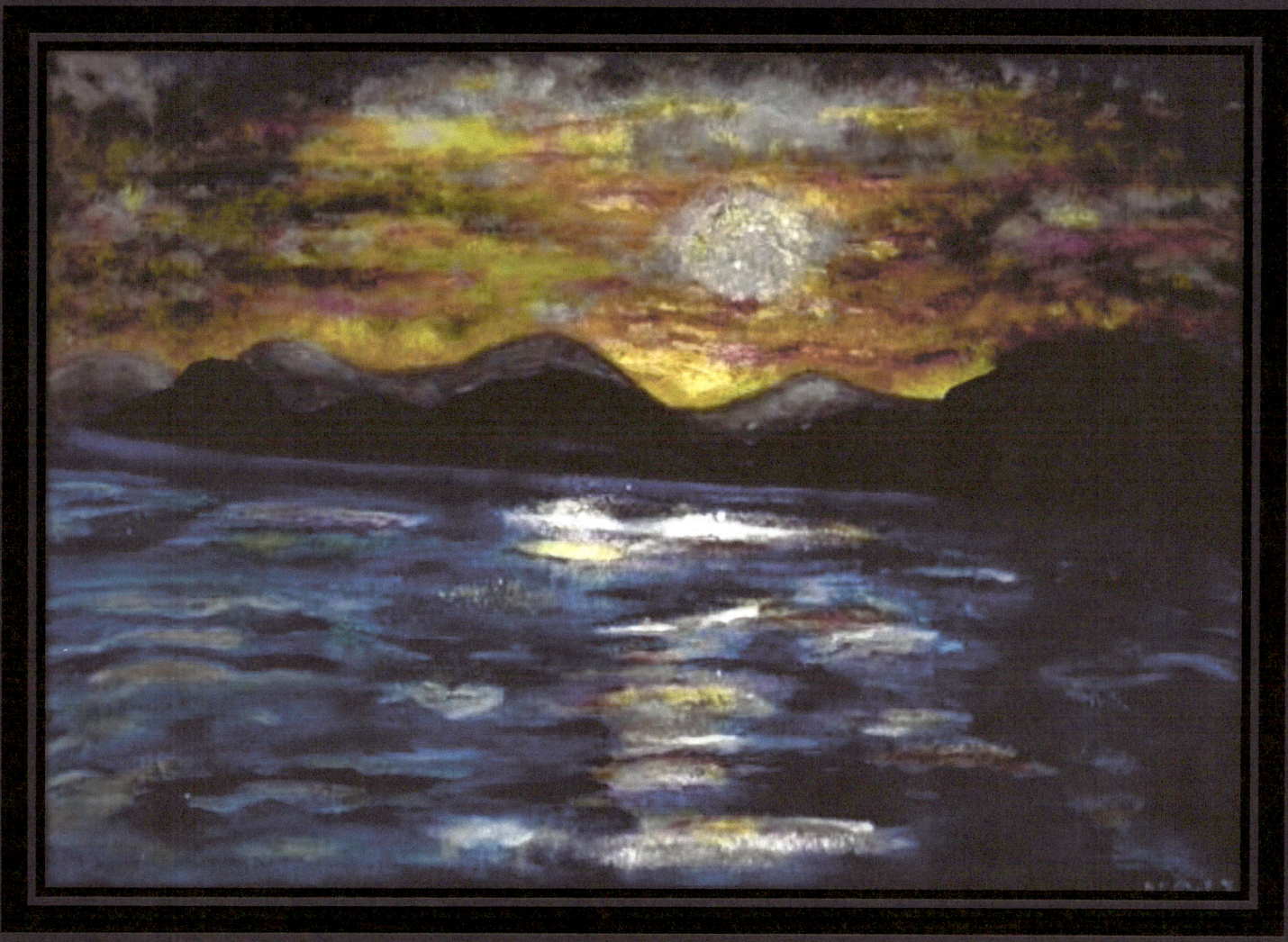

Fantasy

**In the sinking of earth's light
Two breaths became one.**

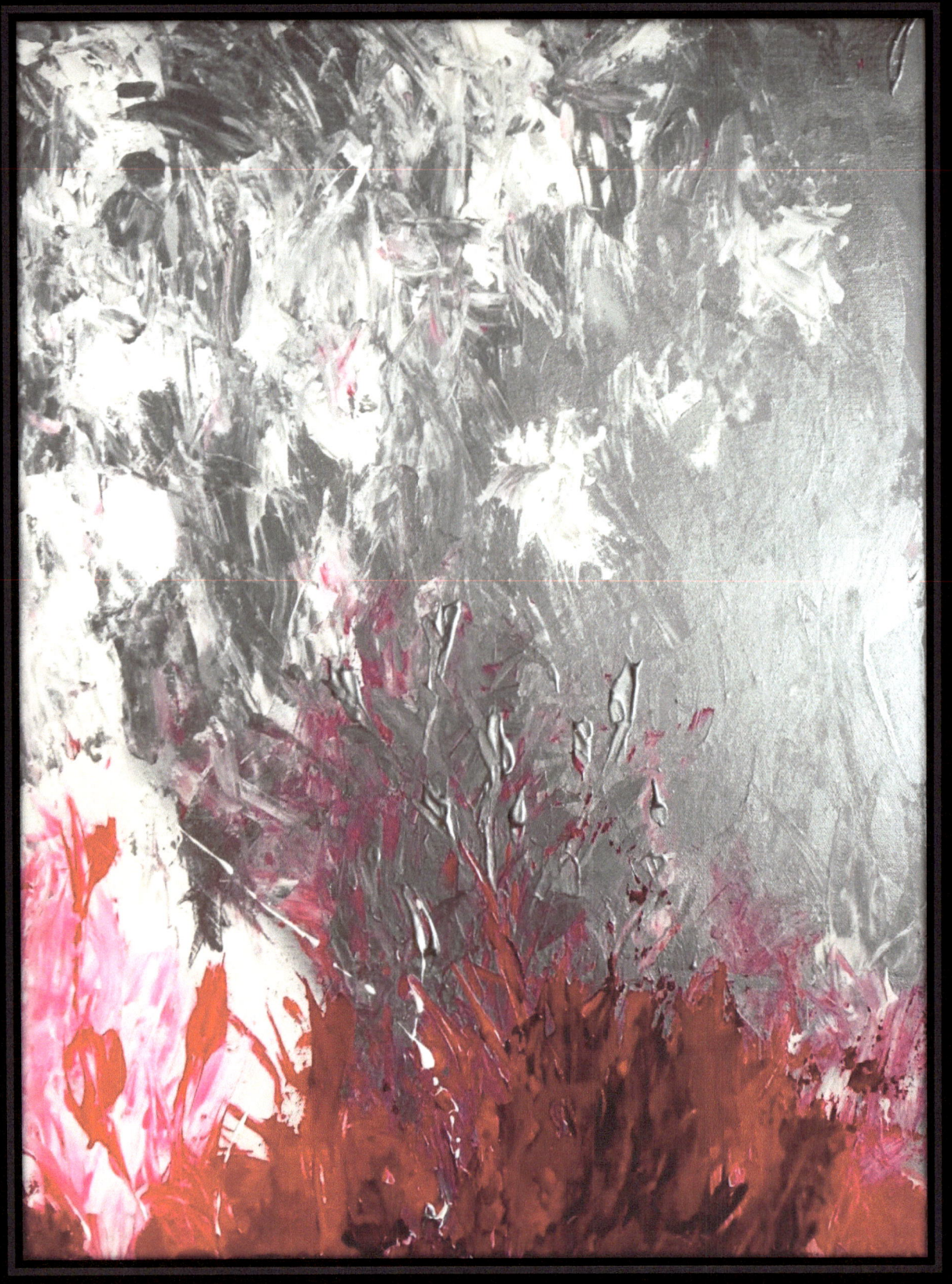

Joy

Touching the lines of lust, and depths of love
Curling deep beneath the arrows of fear
Driving, with and without direction.
The simplest instinct worth following

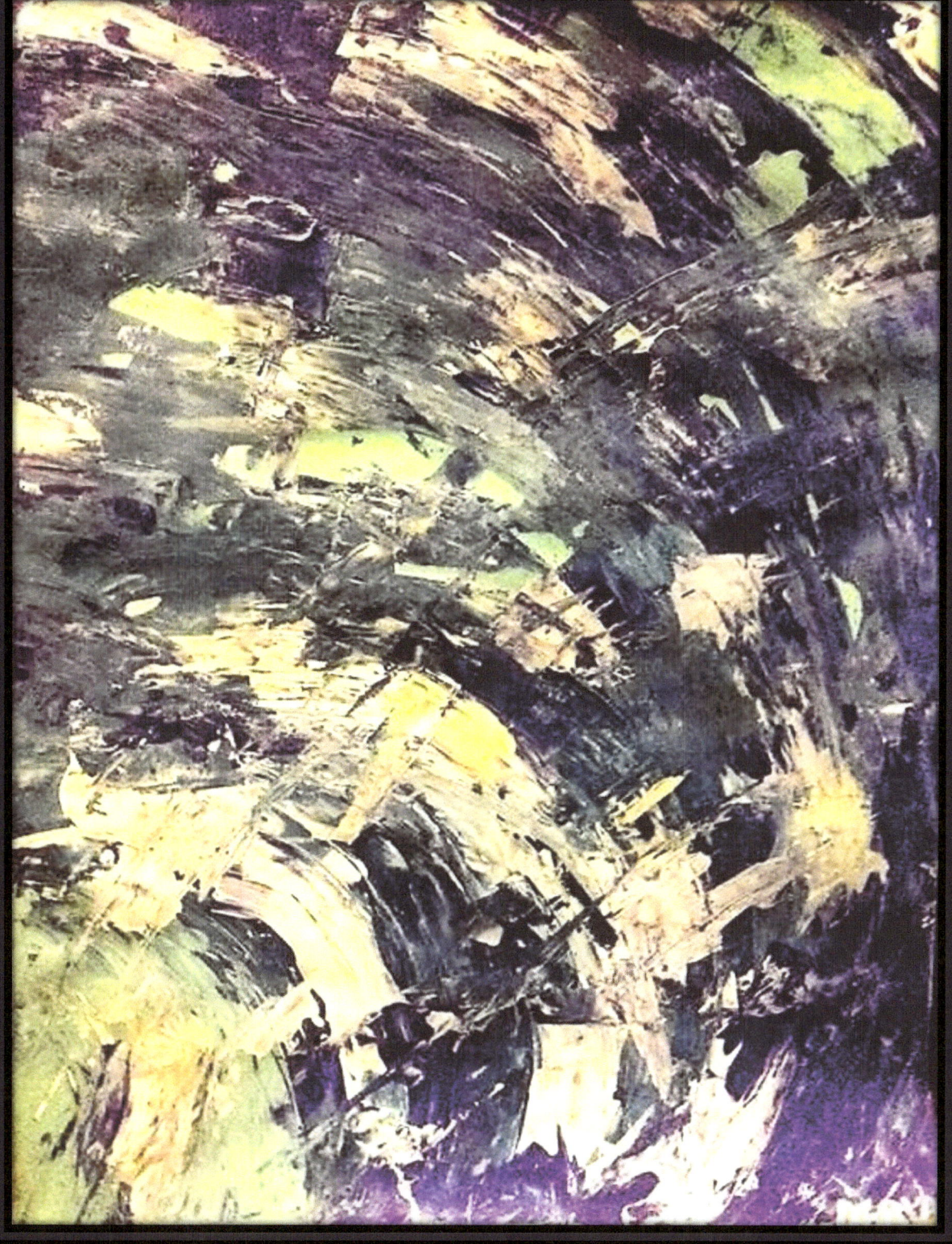

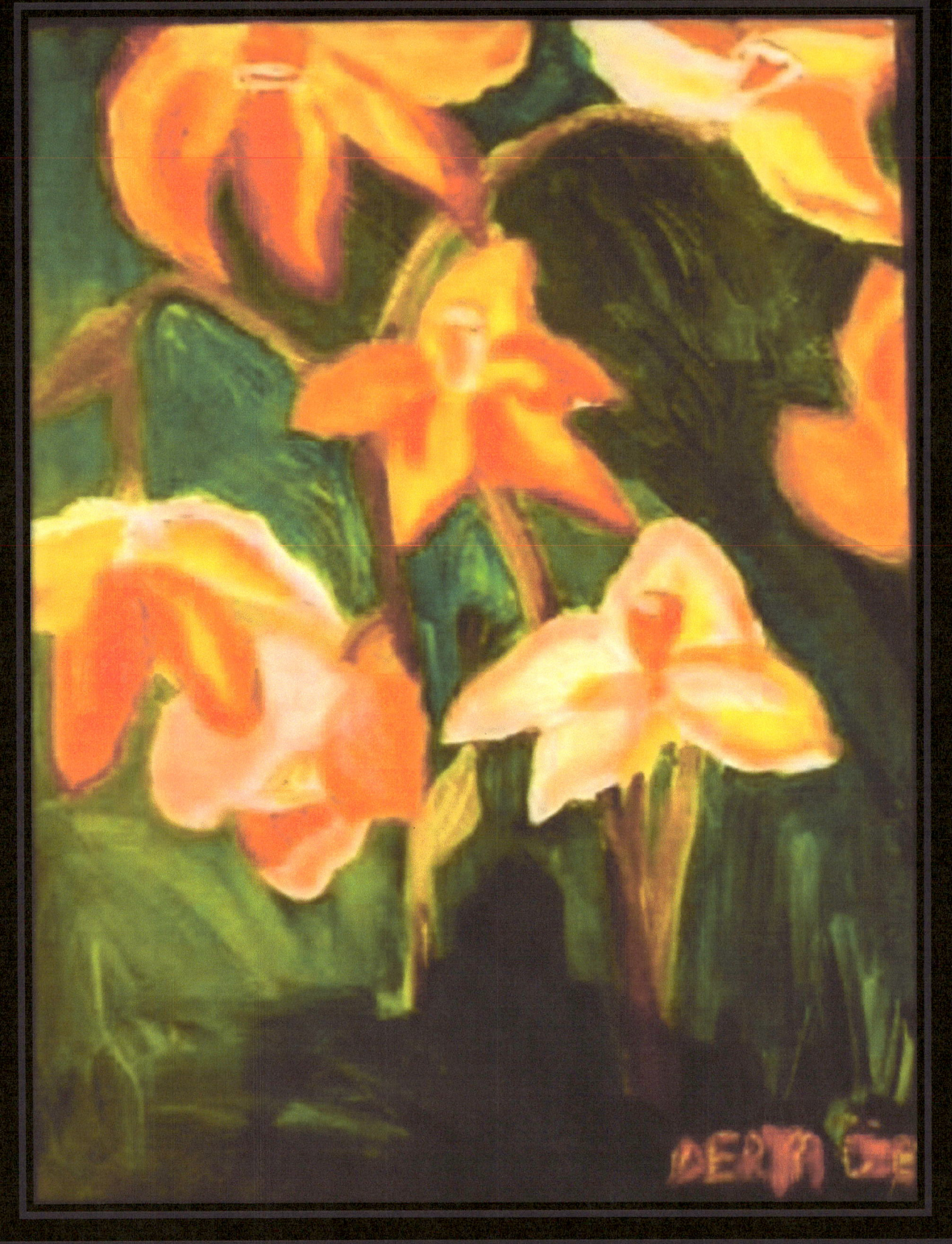

Garden of lovers

They were of the same reflection
Looking into each other,
Feeling more.
Knowing less.

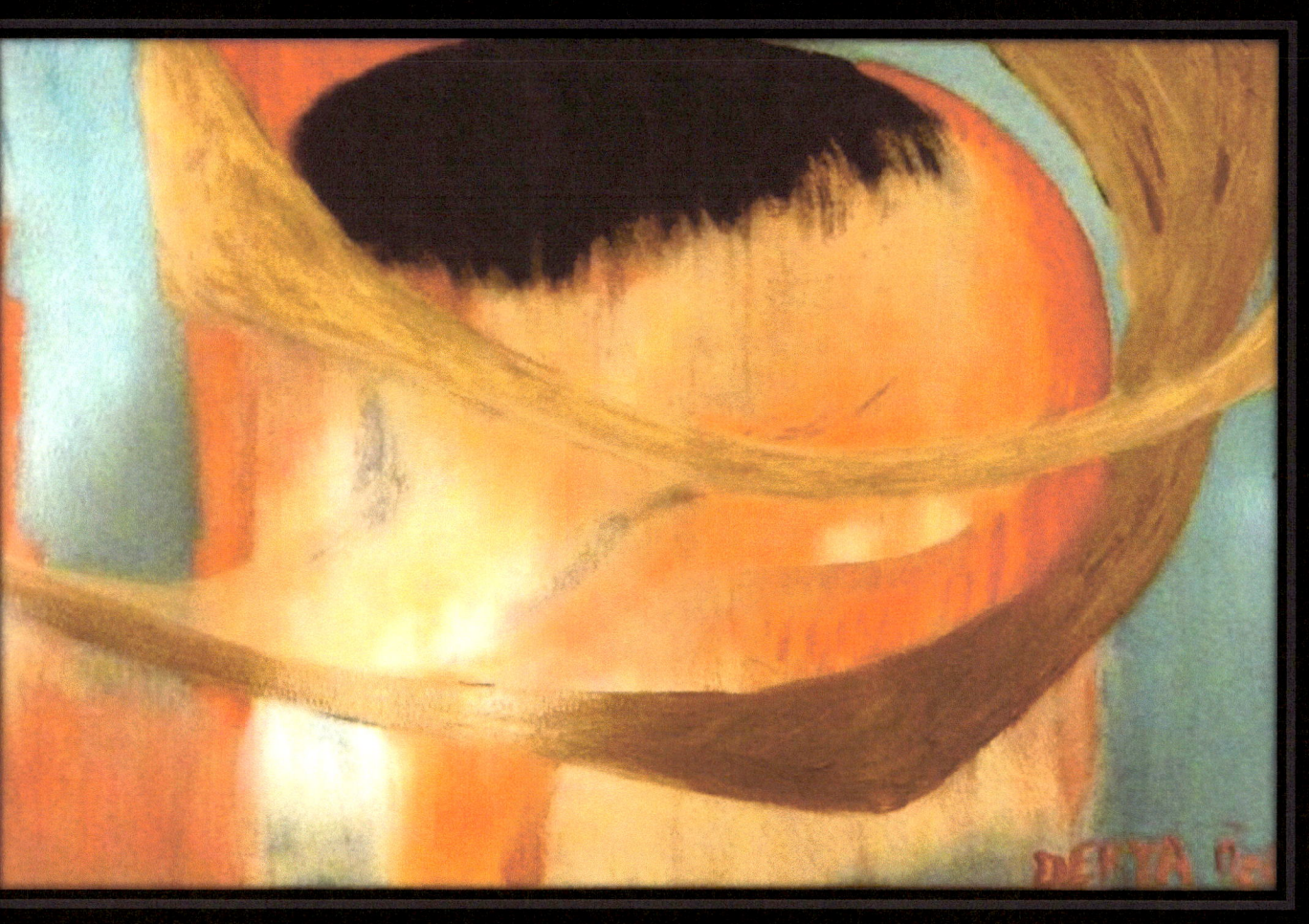

To hold

Bestowed in each other's arms
One learns how not to be

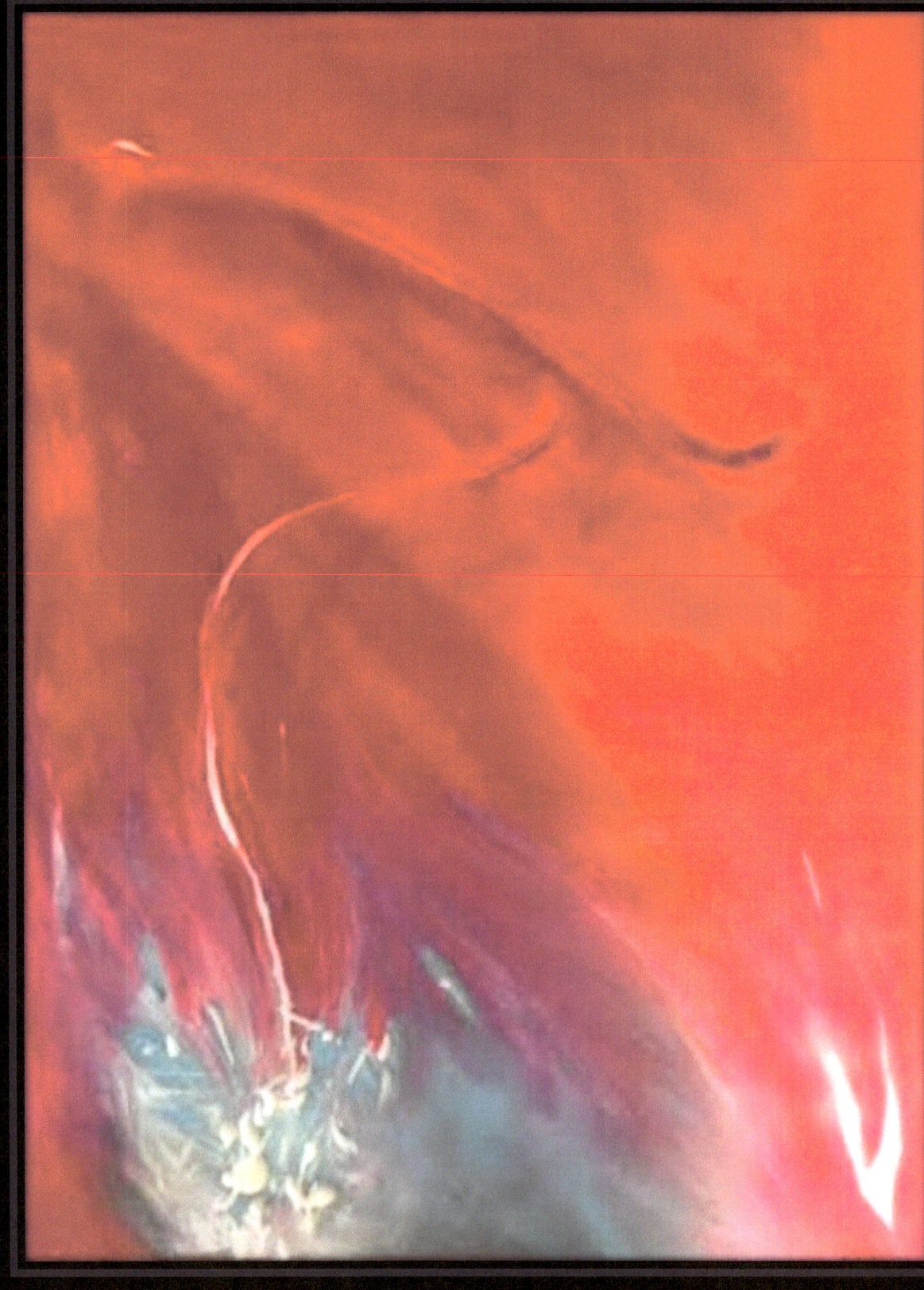

Dance

She, a fire
He, a still river

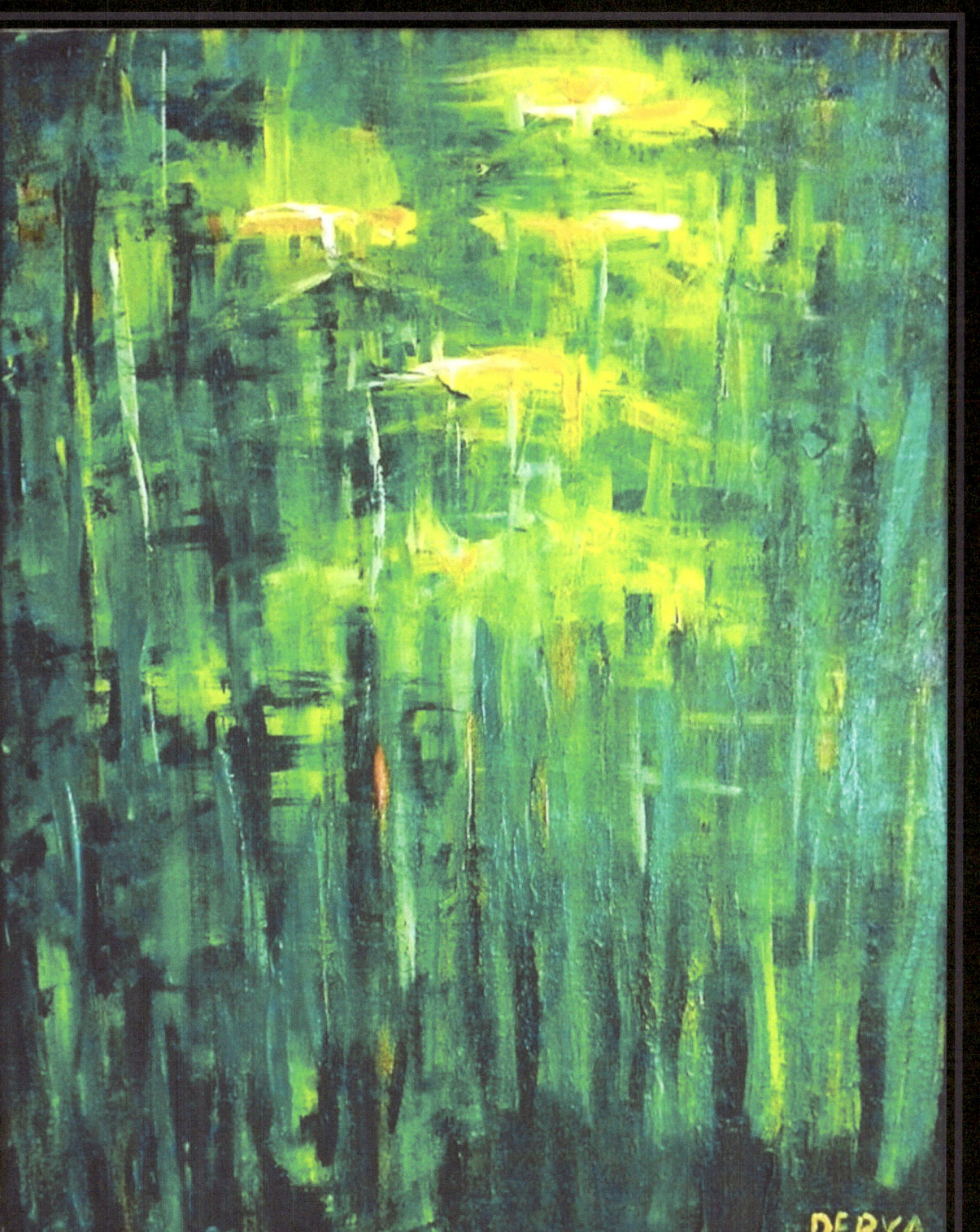

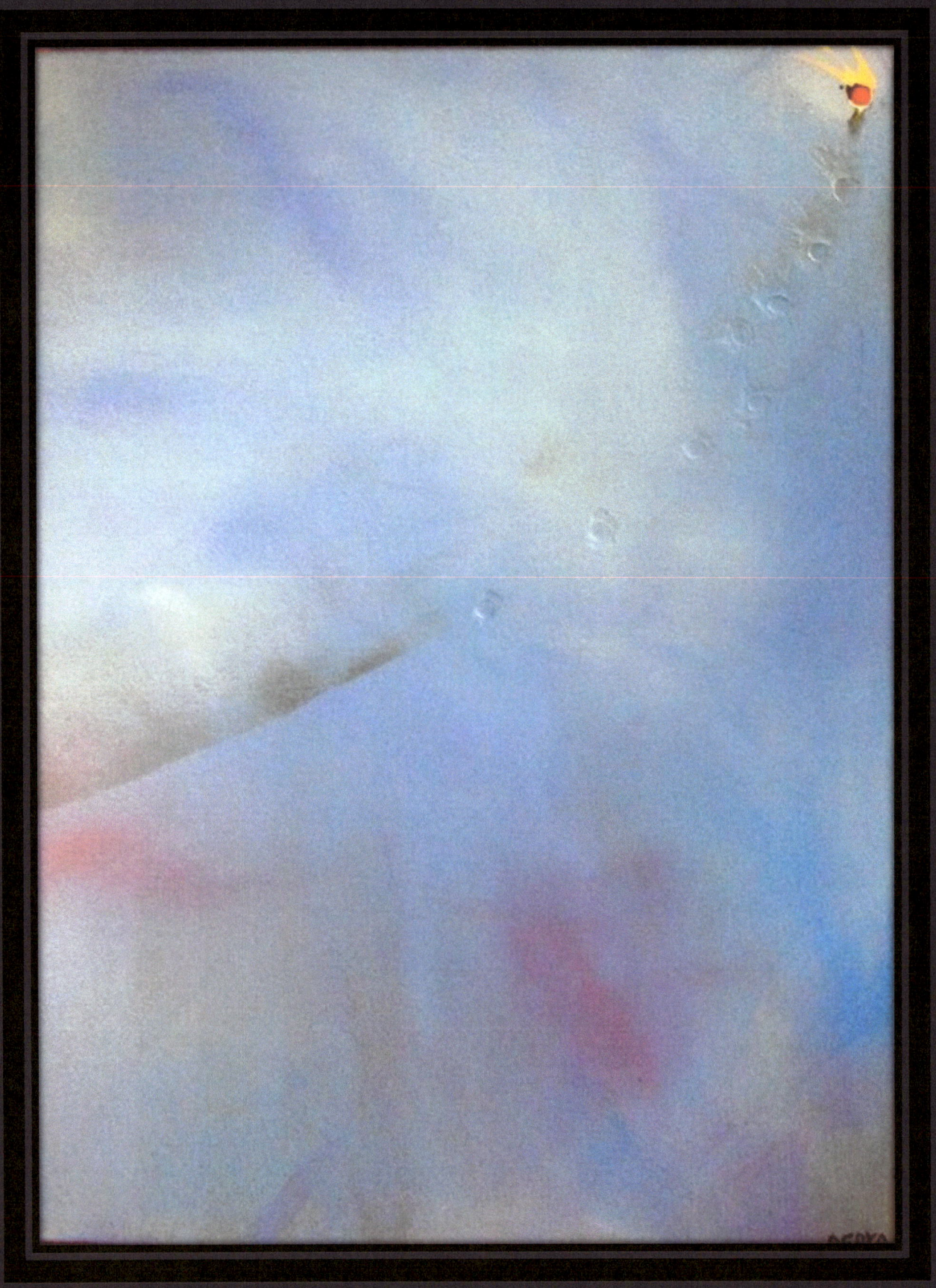

Eagle chaser

She ran after her wings

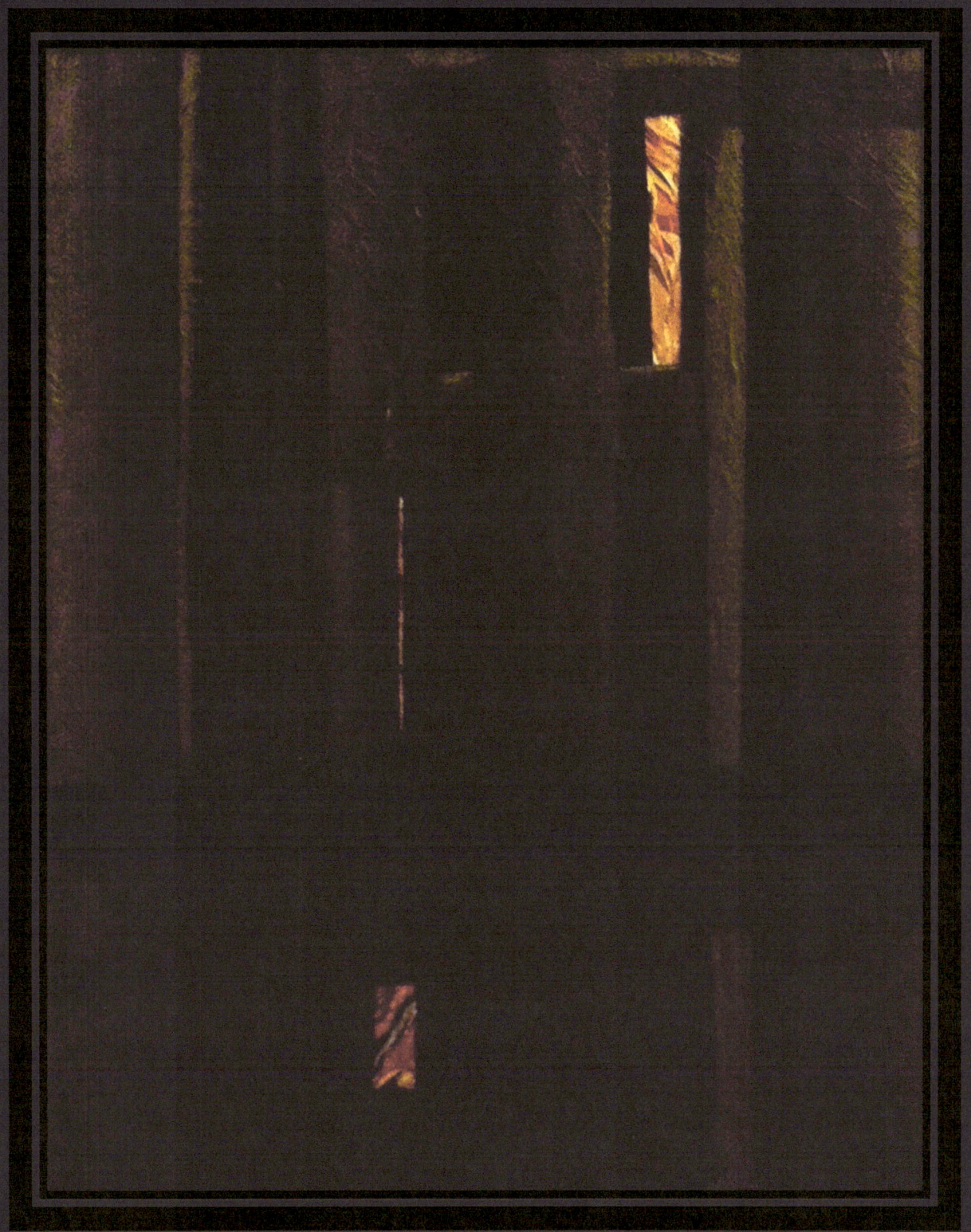

The Veils of Time

Beyond the shadows of the past.
And the darkness within the present.
A light remains within. Guiding your timing.

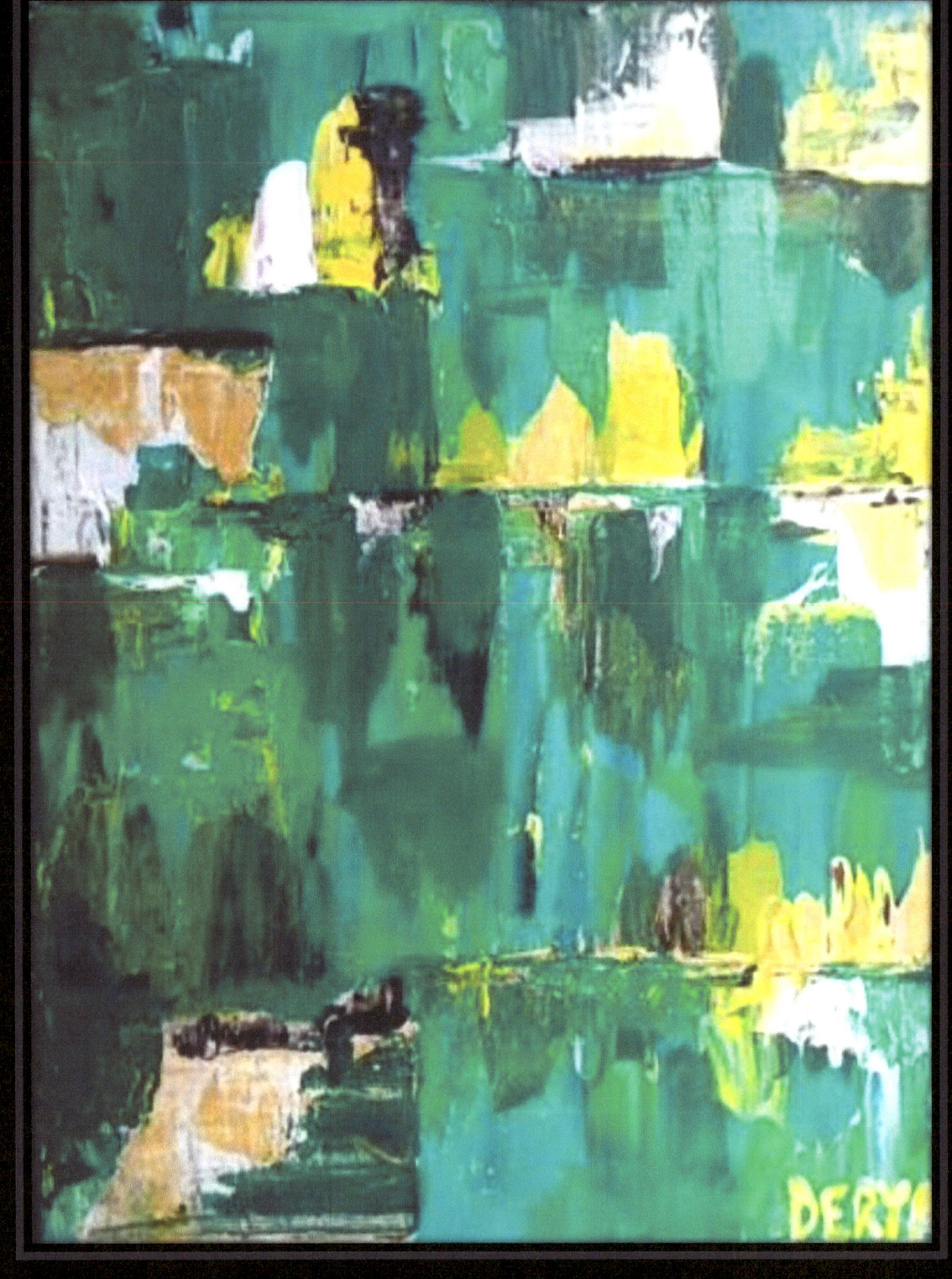

Reflections

On a rock
Half exposed to the heavens
Half sunken within elements made of God
It flowed around the pebbles. Behind and in front.
Her gaze followed the trickle.
The splash awakened her.
So she learned, the rock belongs in the water.

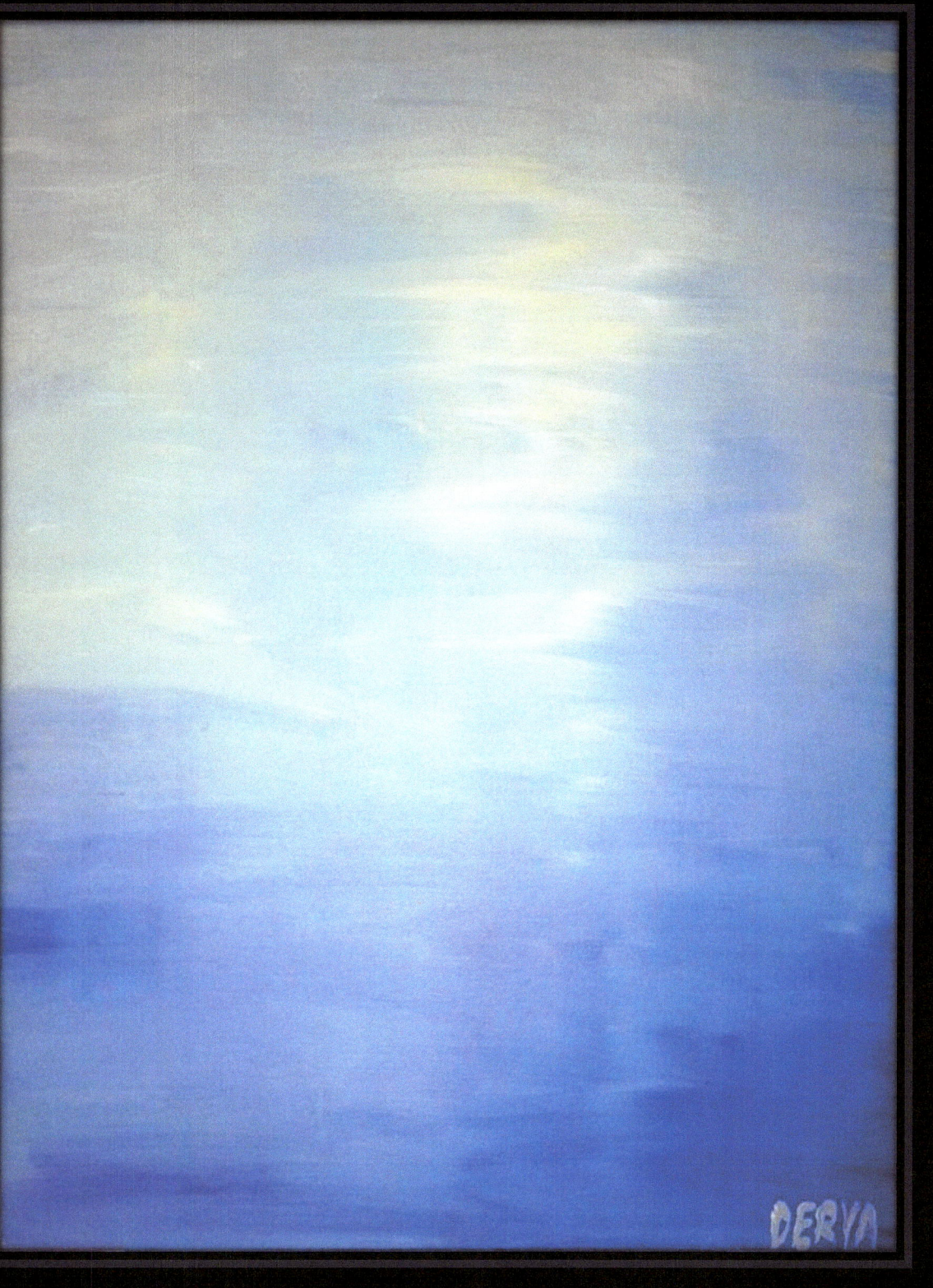

Free

Soaring above the sea,
toward an endless horizon.
Leaving trails
Of sounds,
Made of waves
Beneath.

Surrendering

Eyes caught
By the blink.
They were,
Being without knowing

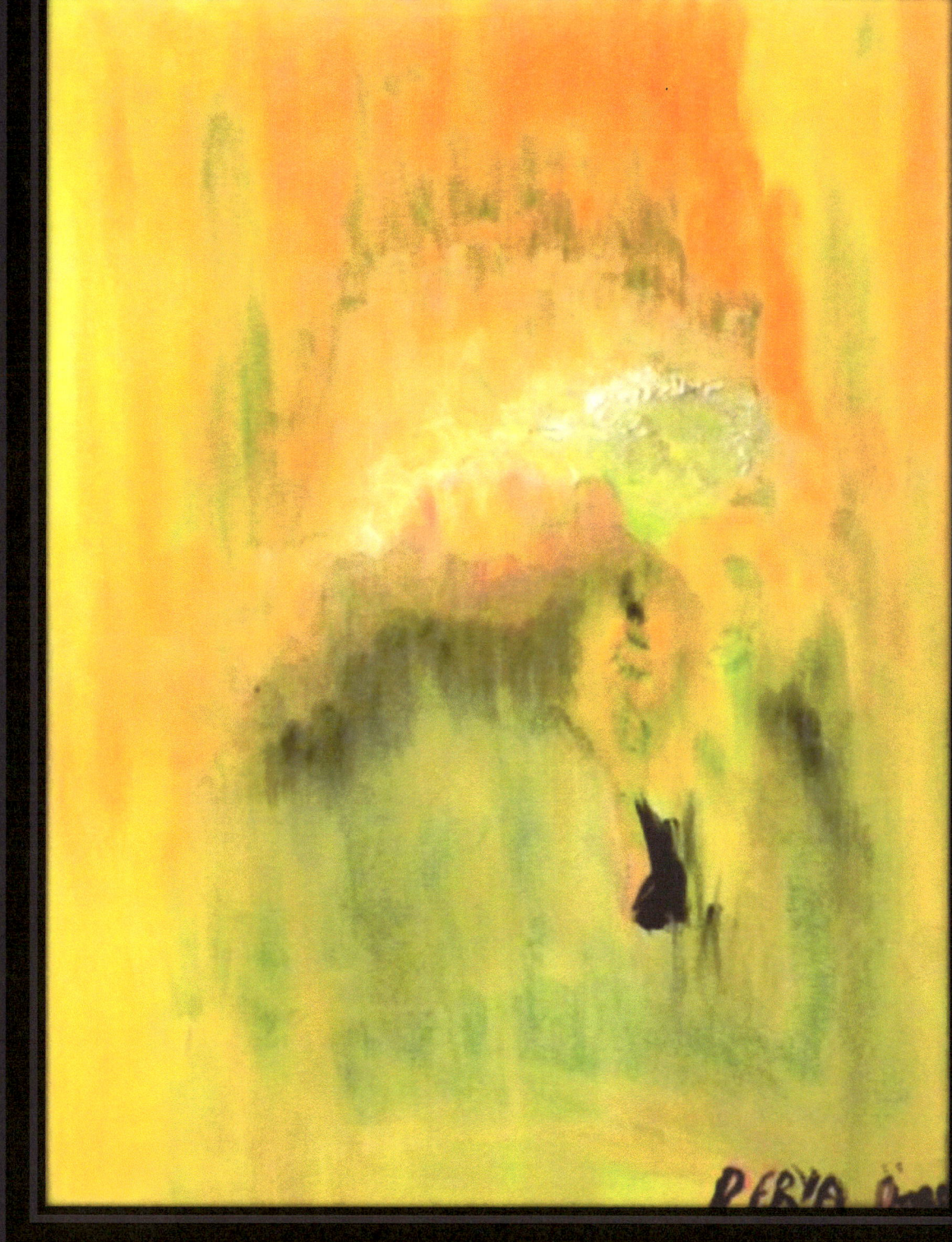

Instinct

An urge in all of us
drives consuming
and desiring,
to be consumed.
Both are as futile,
as it is not.

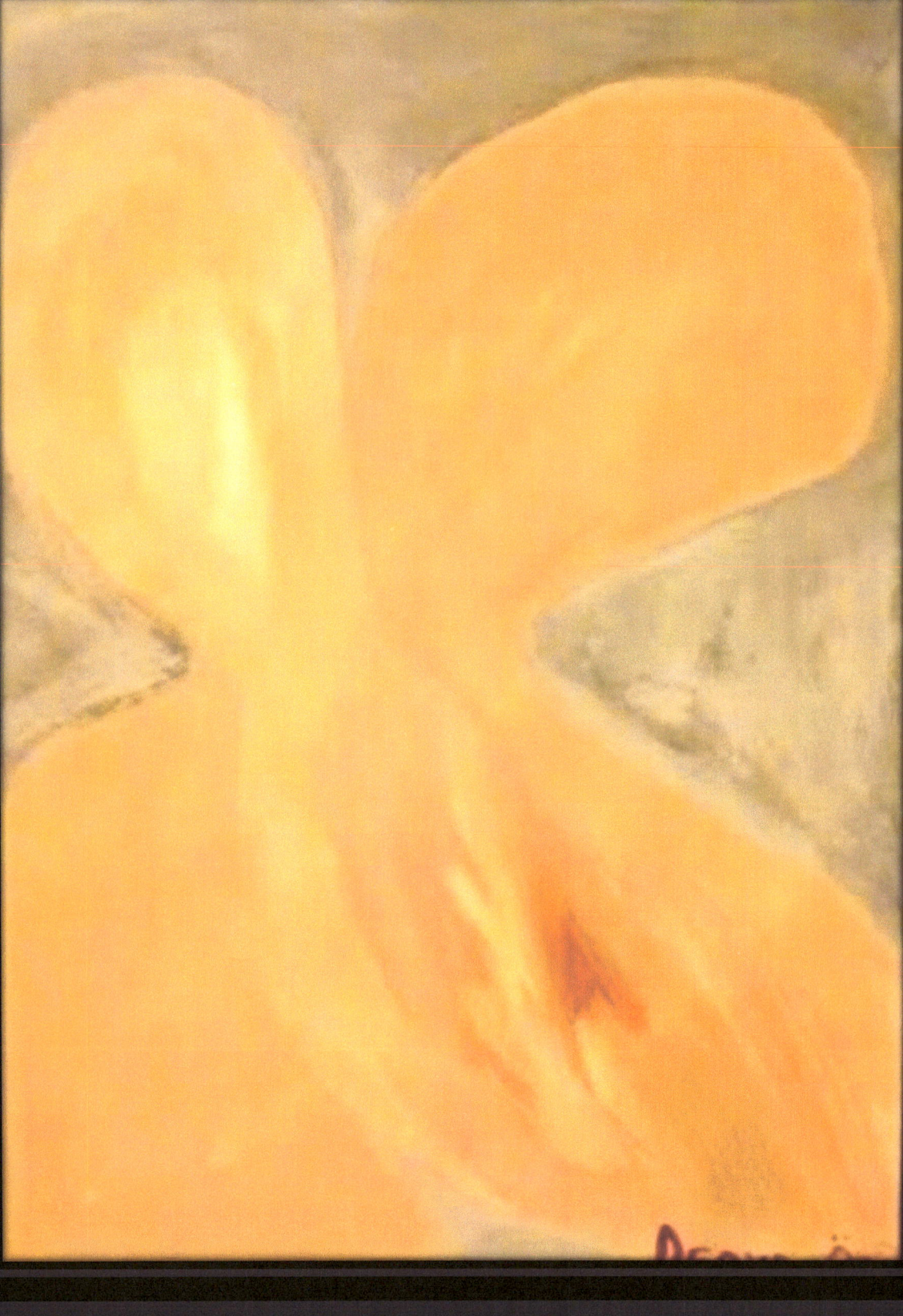

Oneness

The way.

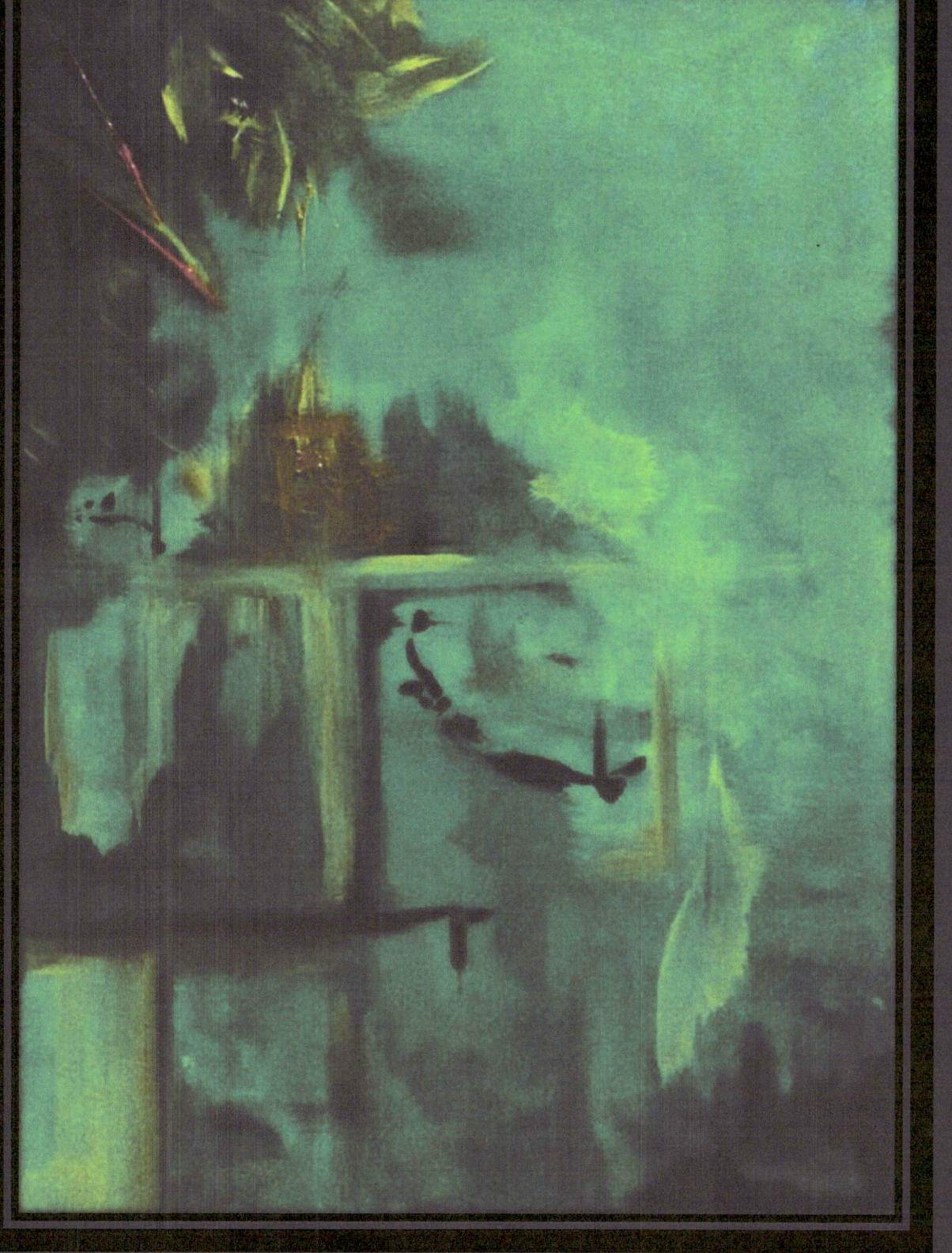

Life

Birth, is aggressive.
Life, a dance.
We Laugh, cry, walk, and run. From place to place.
Psyche to spirit. Body to body. We know. We are. Big and Small.

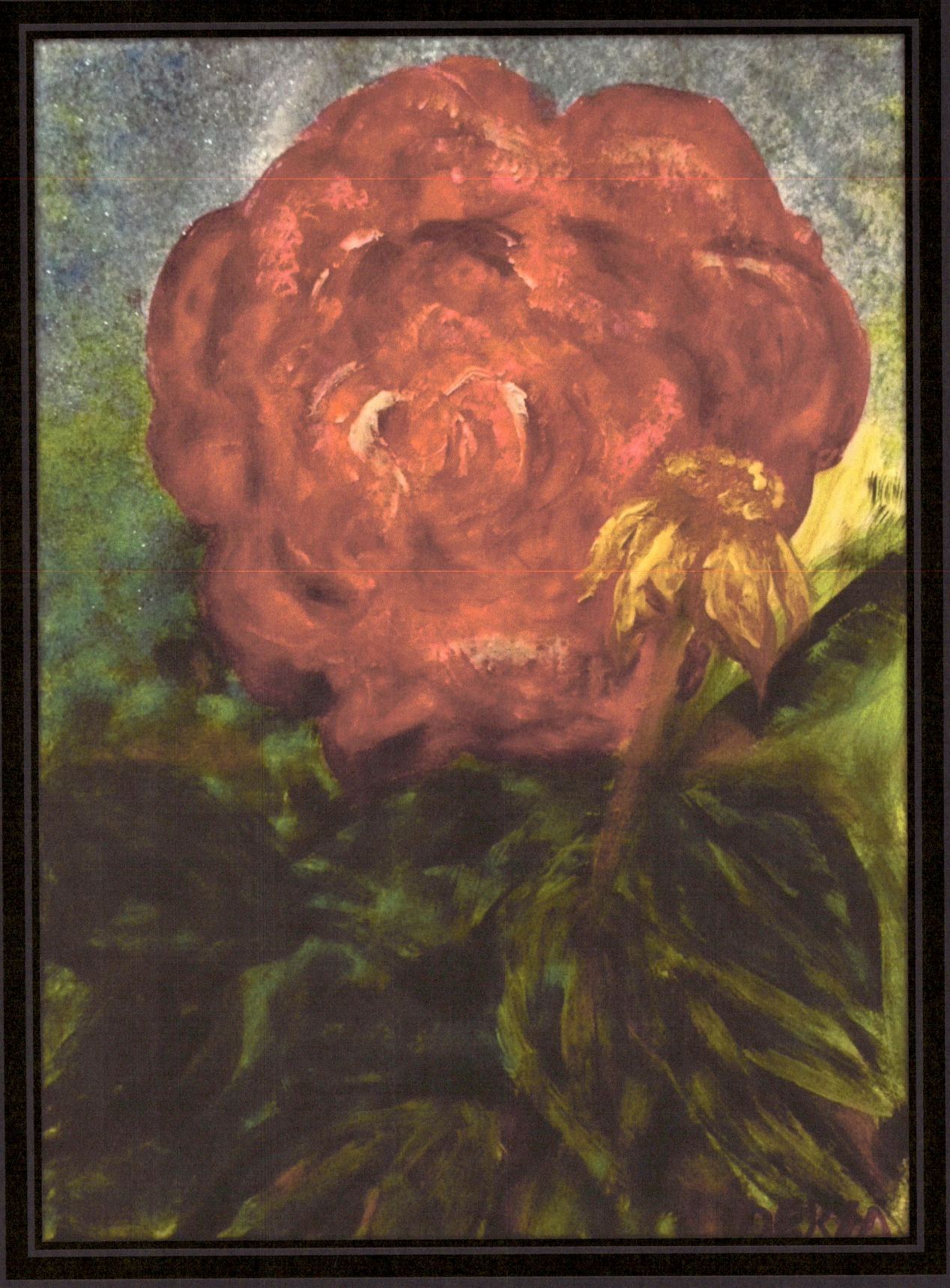

Sığınmak

Curling beneath the wings
Of the one who knows all depths

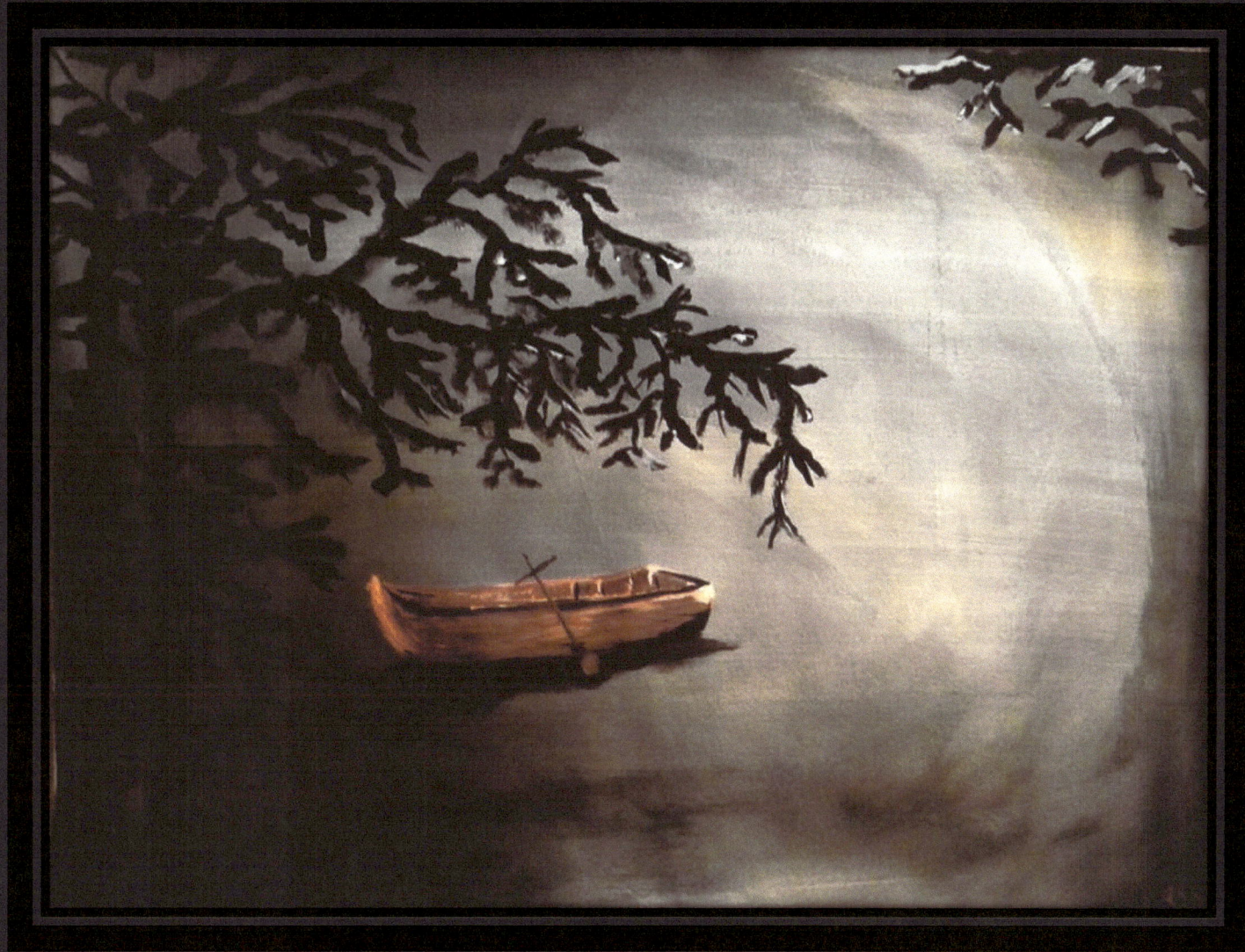

Essence

Silence
is gentle and bold
It speaks when you see
What you've been missing.

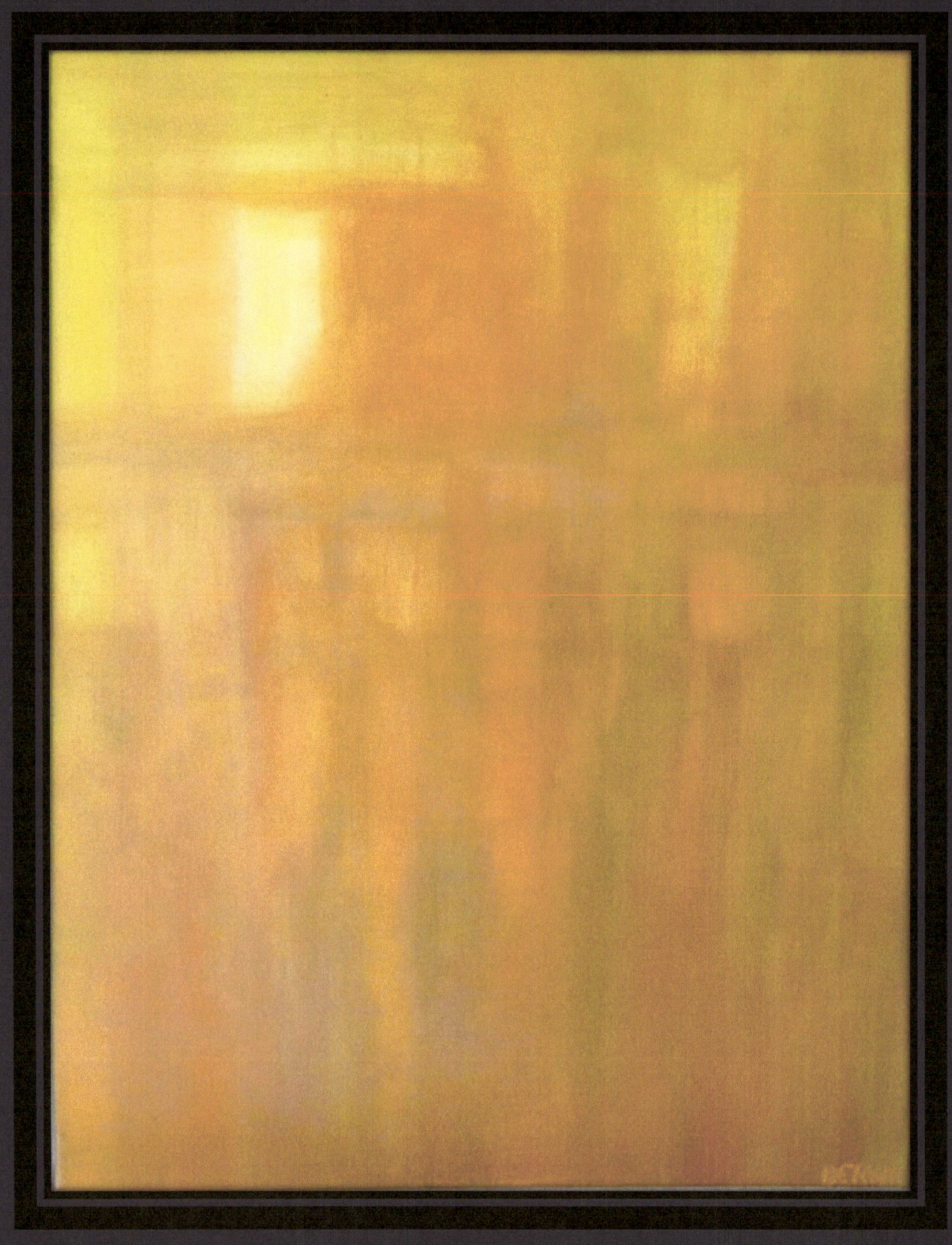

Walls

On a bridge
Right, left, below and above
Civilizations once thrived.

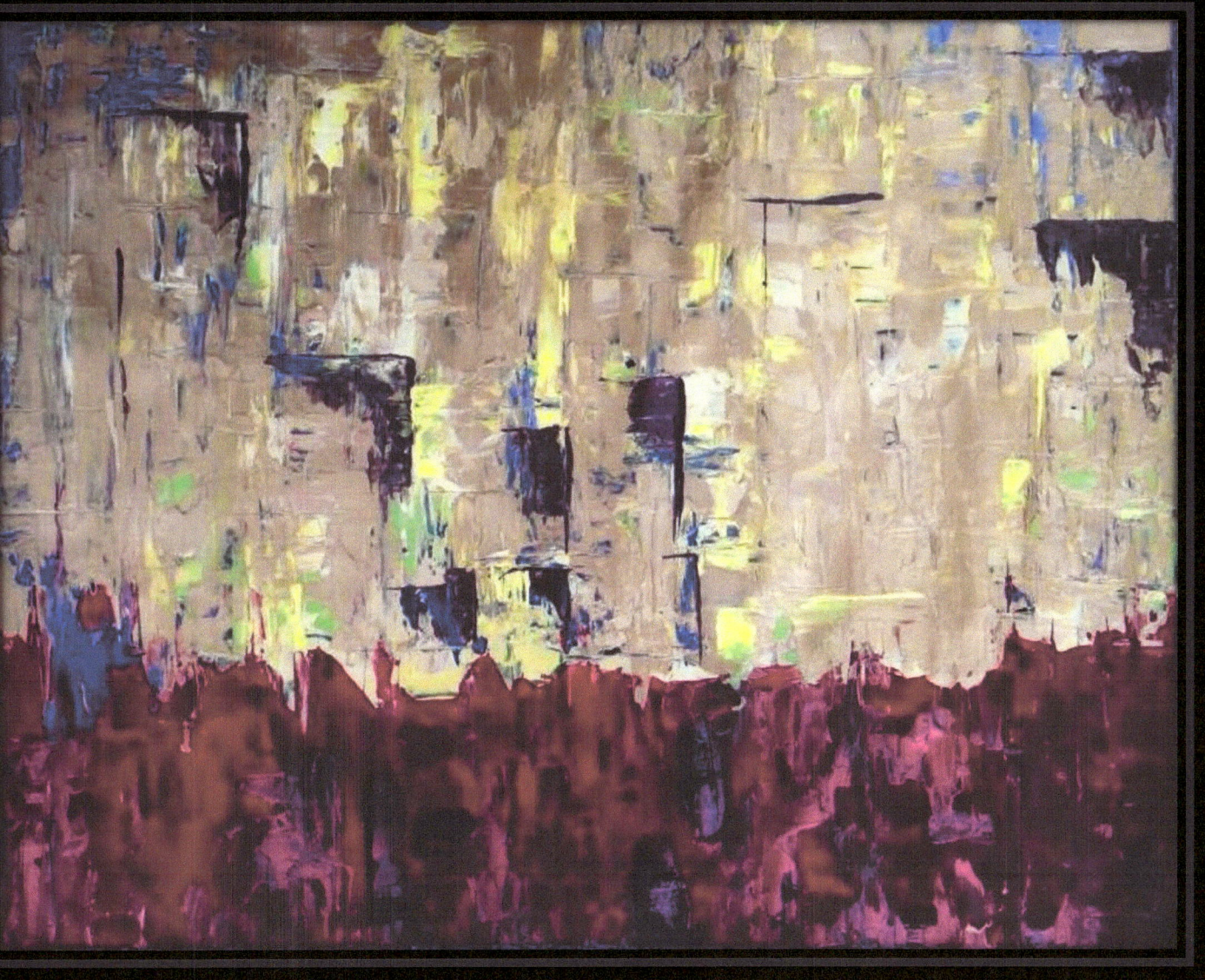

Buildings

They
Stand.
A reminder,
Of permanence
Hoovering.
They judge,
How tall you have become.

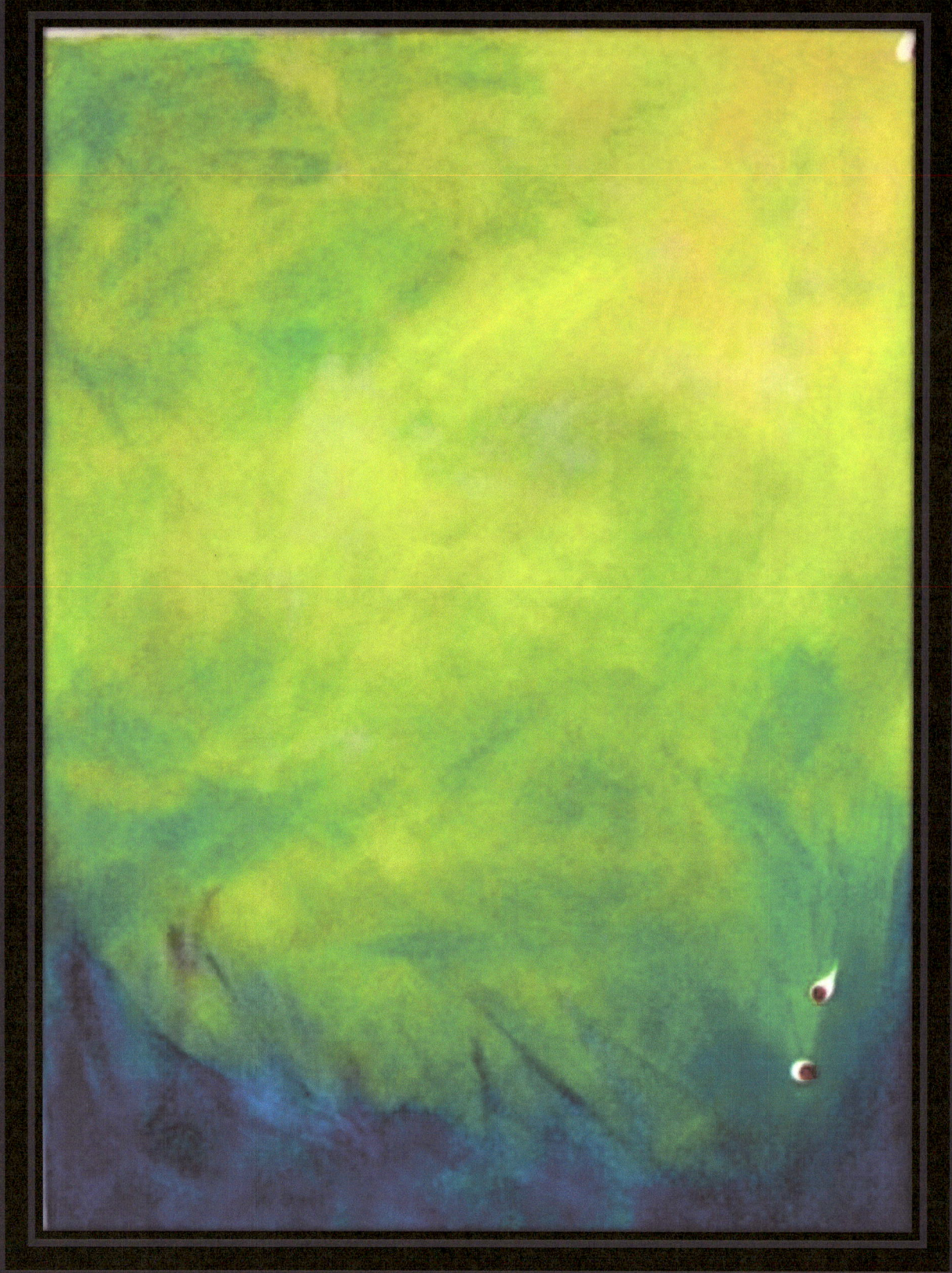

His Pistachio Eyes

Hues of yellow, green, blue.
They smile from within and afar.
like a wave,
capturing her bronze
they swirl
Till two become one

The Wound

A pain swirls on the brink
Of your flesh.
Vast it is. And it likes to flirt.
Half dead, half alive. Your consciousness.
Trying to grasp a breath.

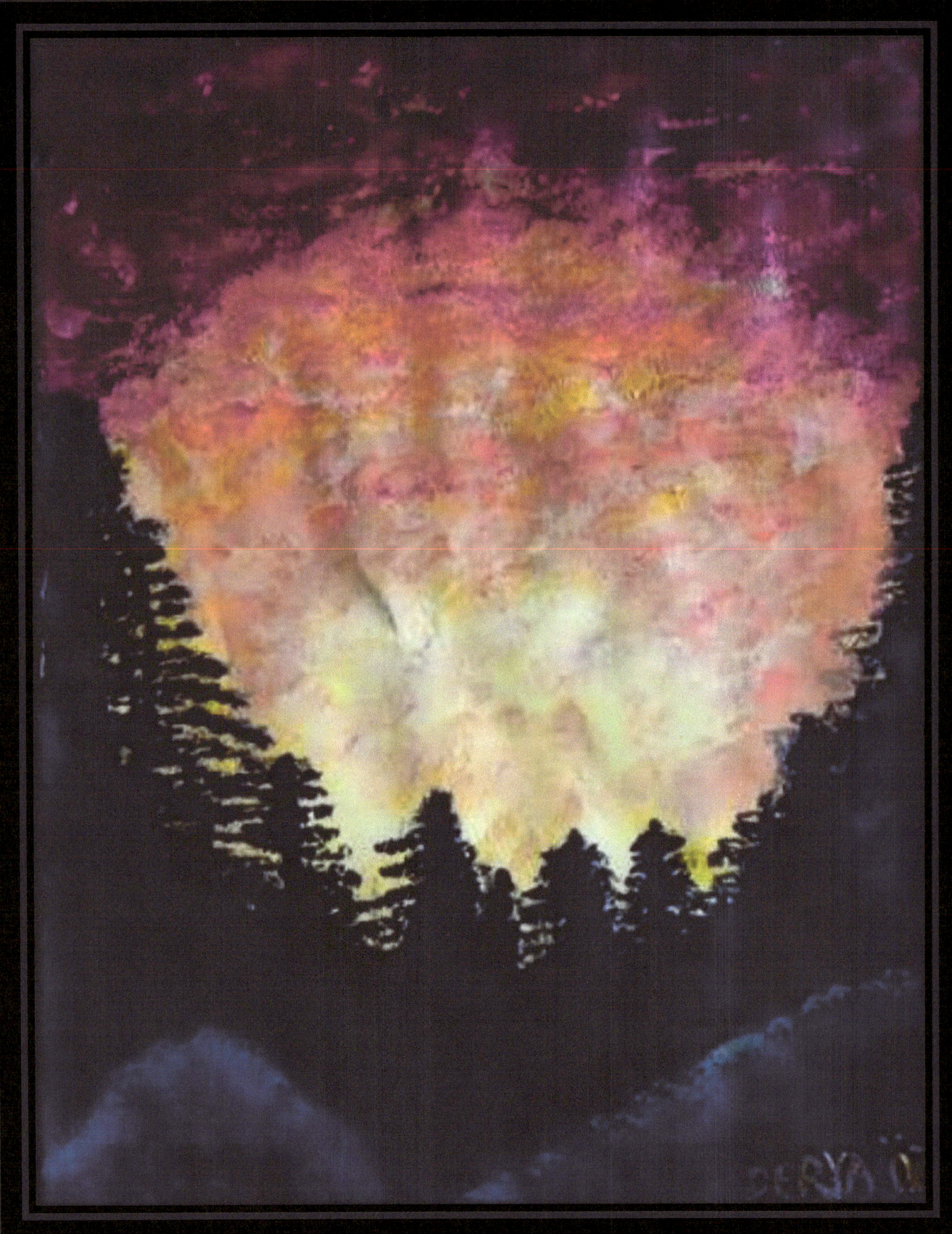

Projecting

Thoughts about a future
carved into the imagination
Fueled by the suns rest
It was an imagination.

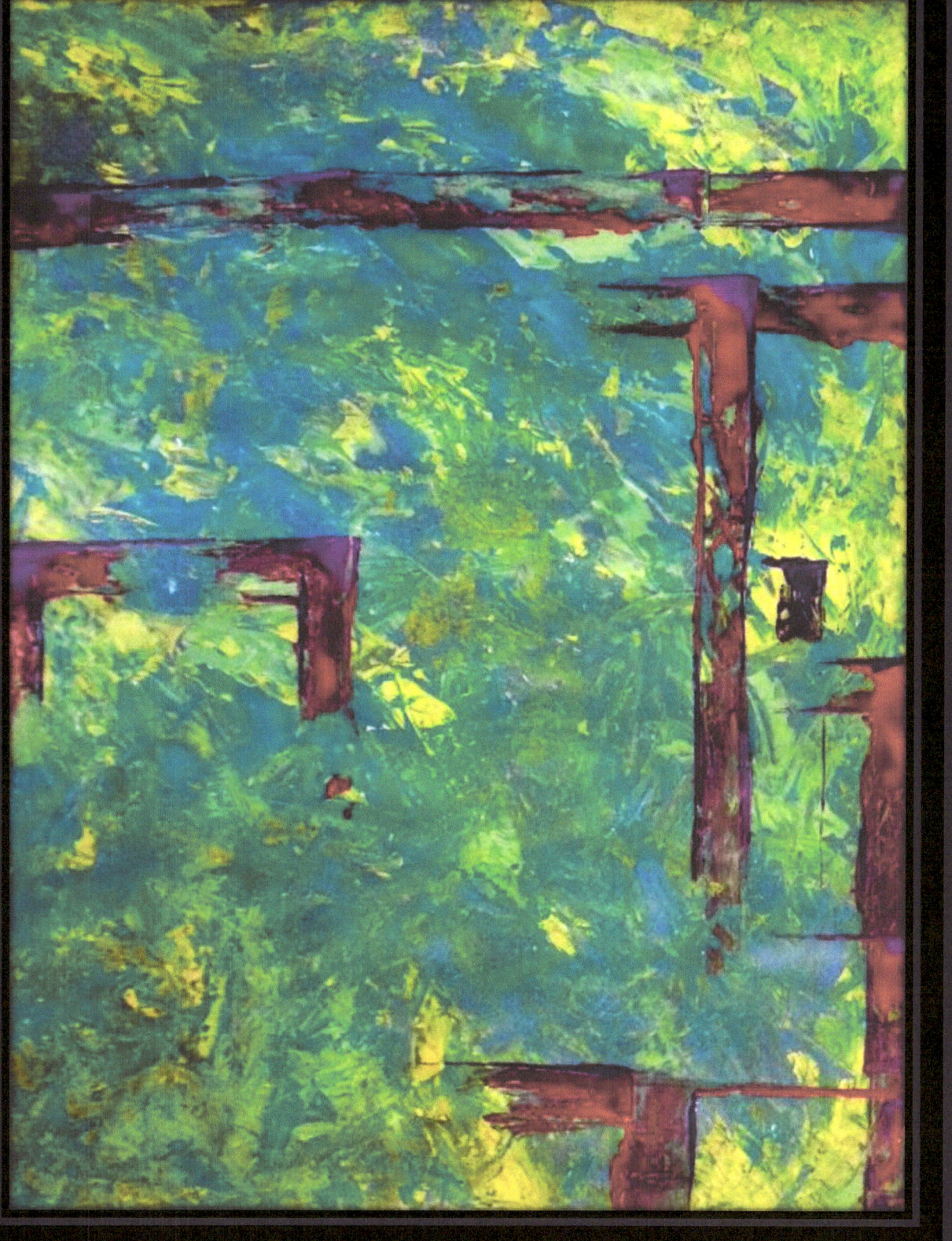

Bridges

He walked on bridges
Which stood
on still waters.
Stirred what settled.
That which was over
Yet, never begun.

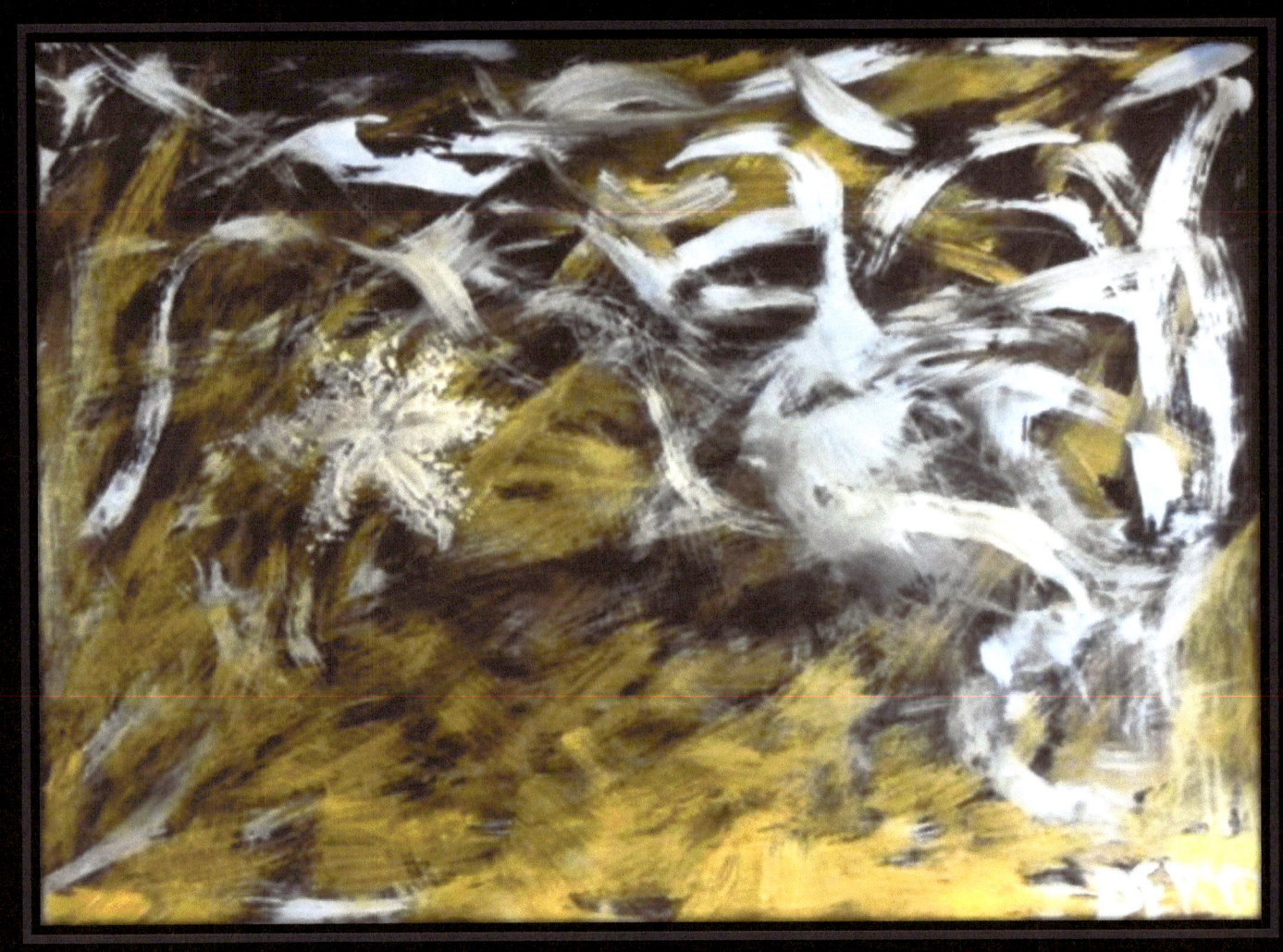

Gazed Upon a Wish

A normal day it was.
Accompanied by a normal walk.
She stumped upon a sight.
First her eyes followed,
Then her feet ,
Captivated by the innocent pleasure.
As if flirting with life.
And pointing at her,
To show how easy it was.
To be happy

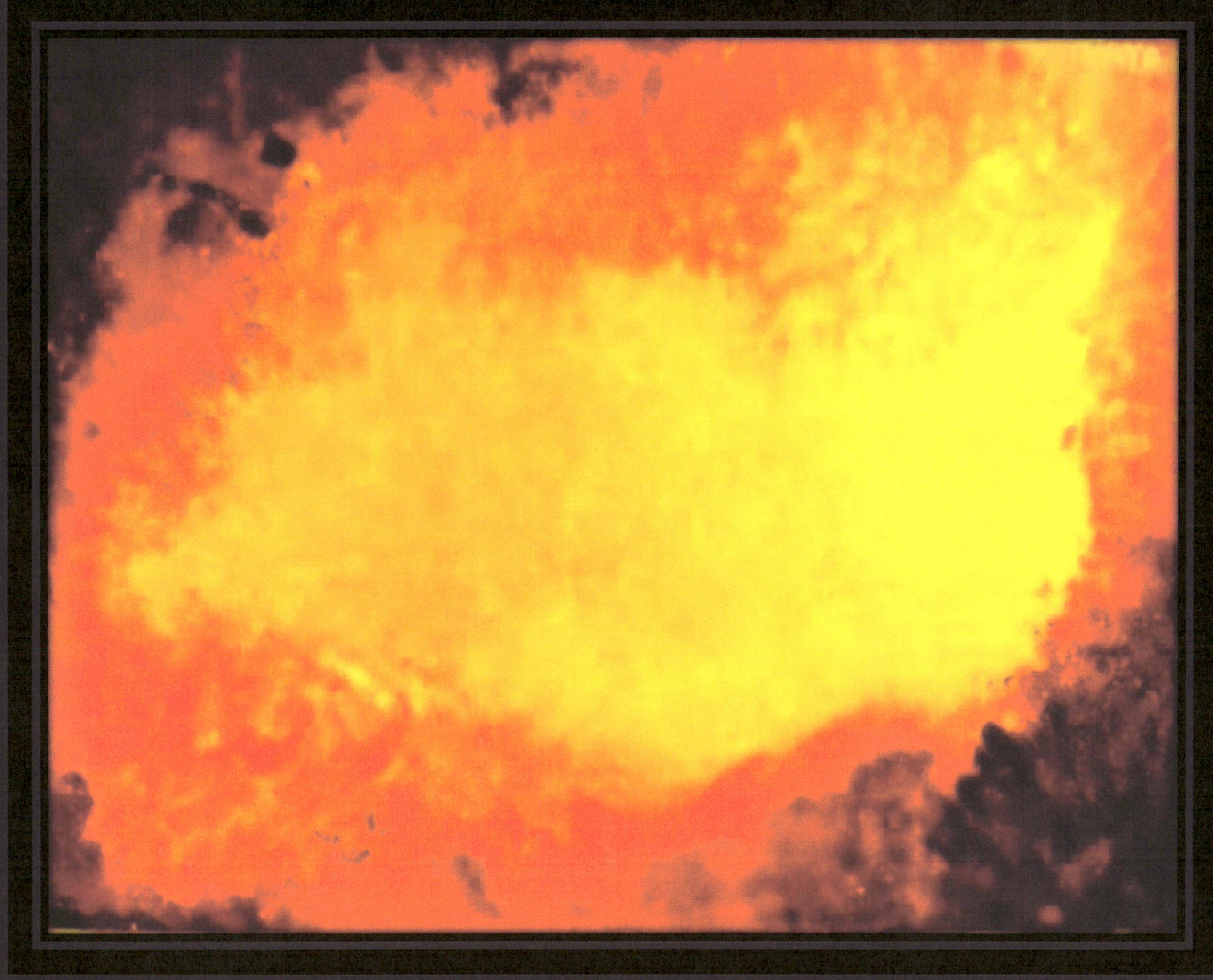

Reaching

In distance
They seek each other
Surrendering
To aches of longing

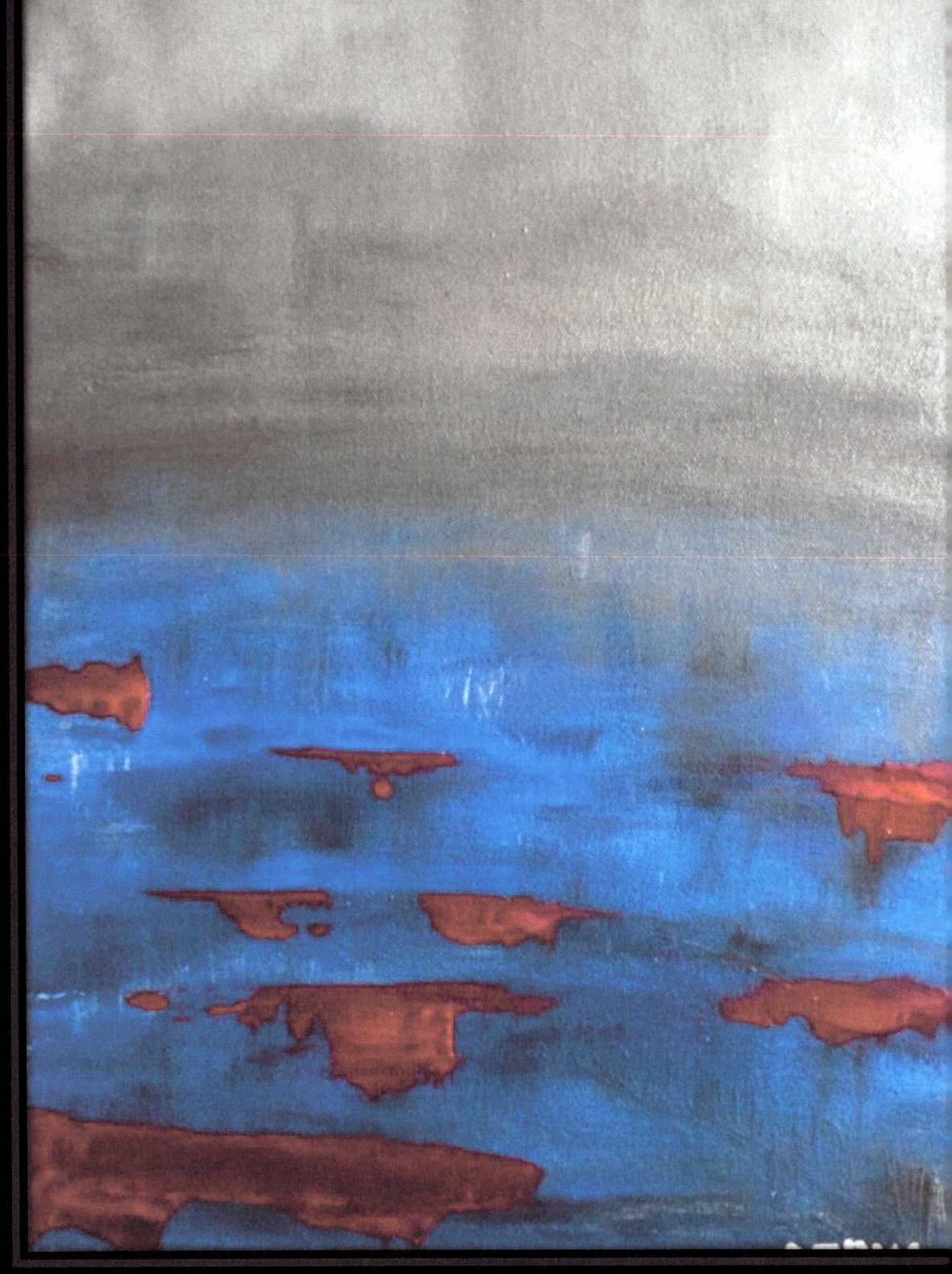

Tezahür

As shadows chase us.
We cast a shade
Reflecting on each other.
Who was the chaser
Who, the chased?

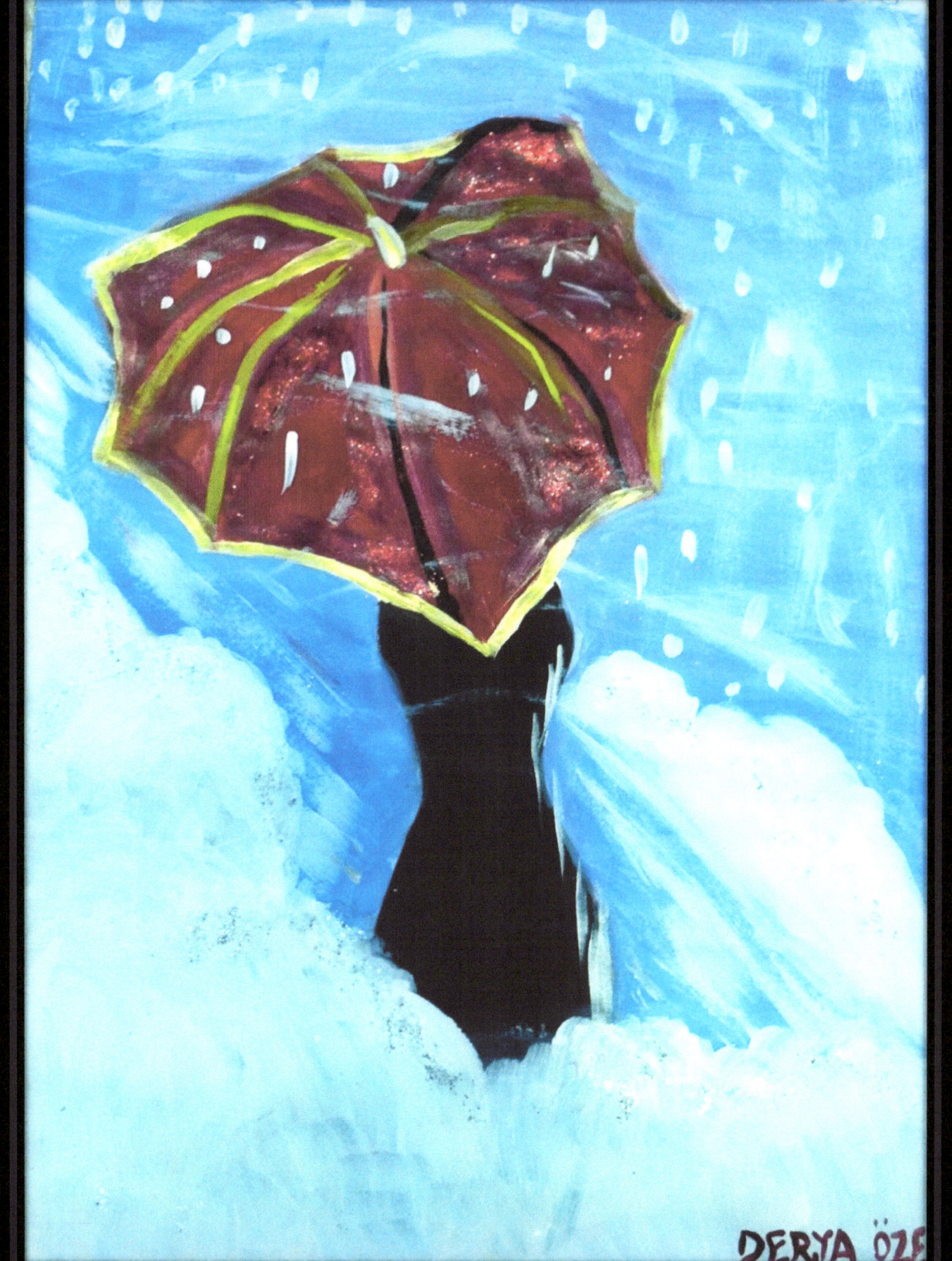

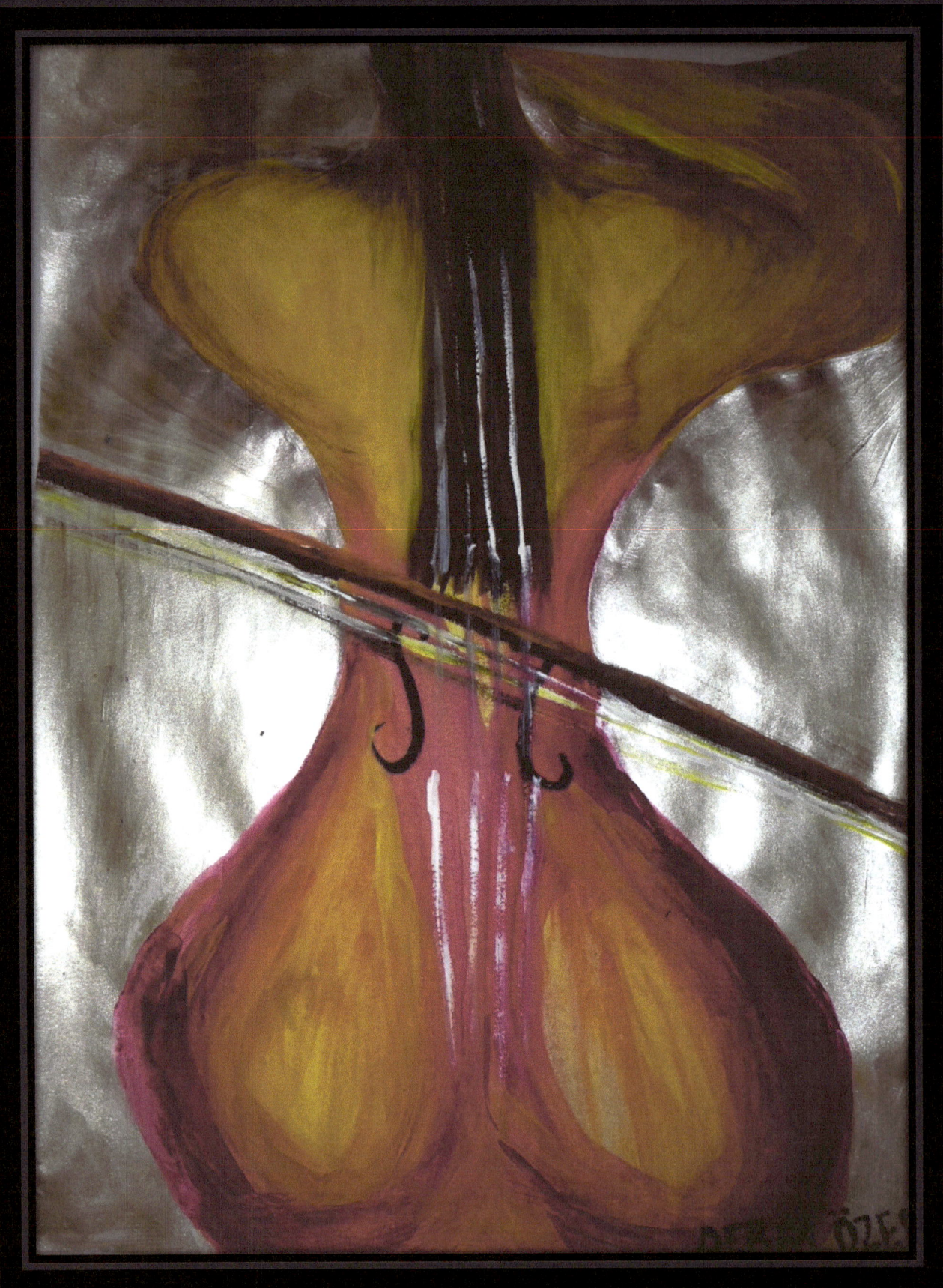

" Hasret "

She cried
With the echo's that played her

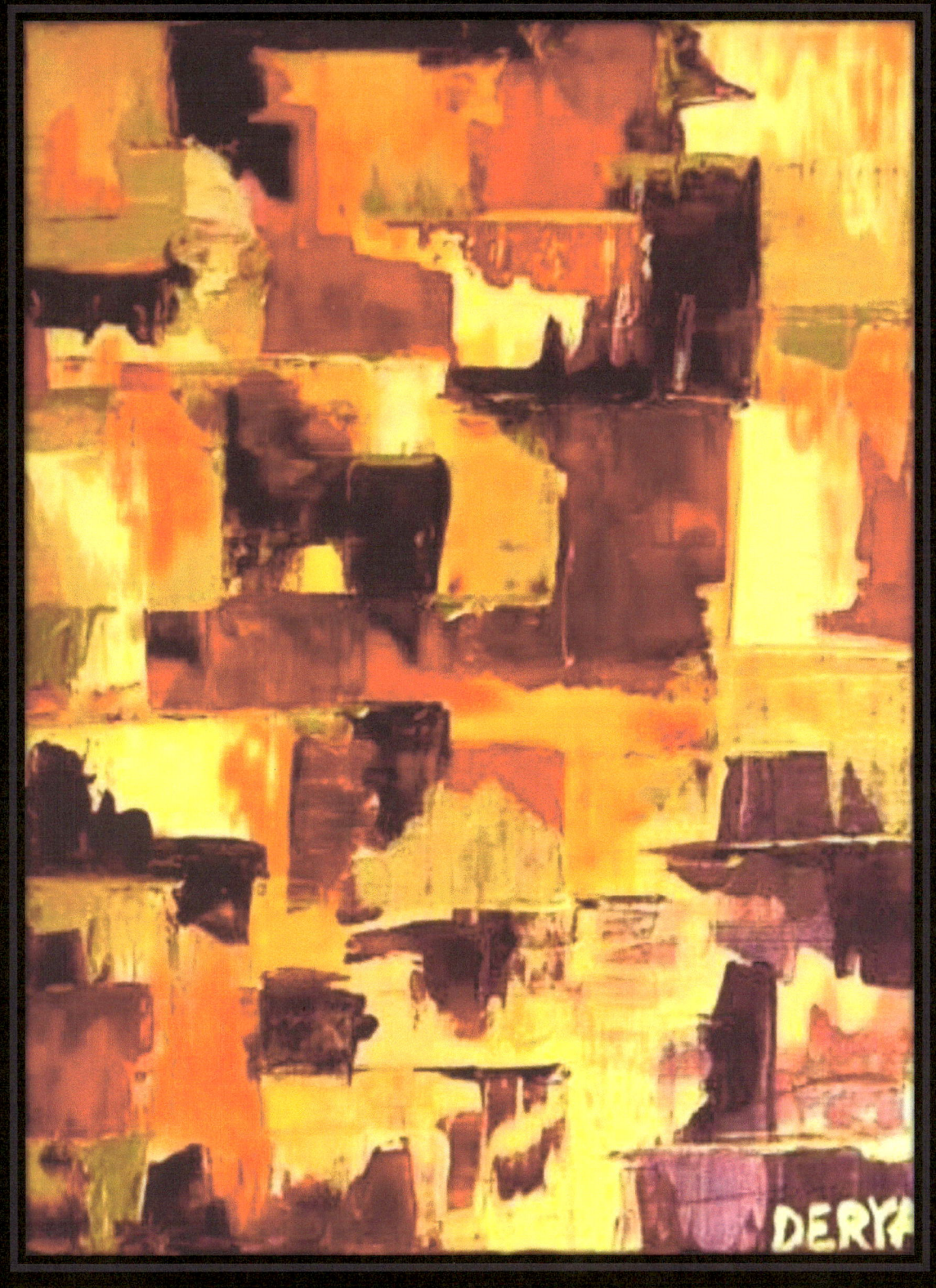

25th Hour

Eye lashes raised
A ray shined into her sight
Her frown
Volted into a lullaby

with earths diamond
She whispered back.
I see you.
You are I, I am you.

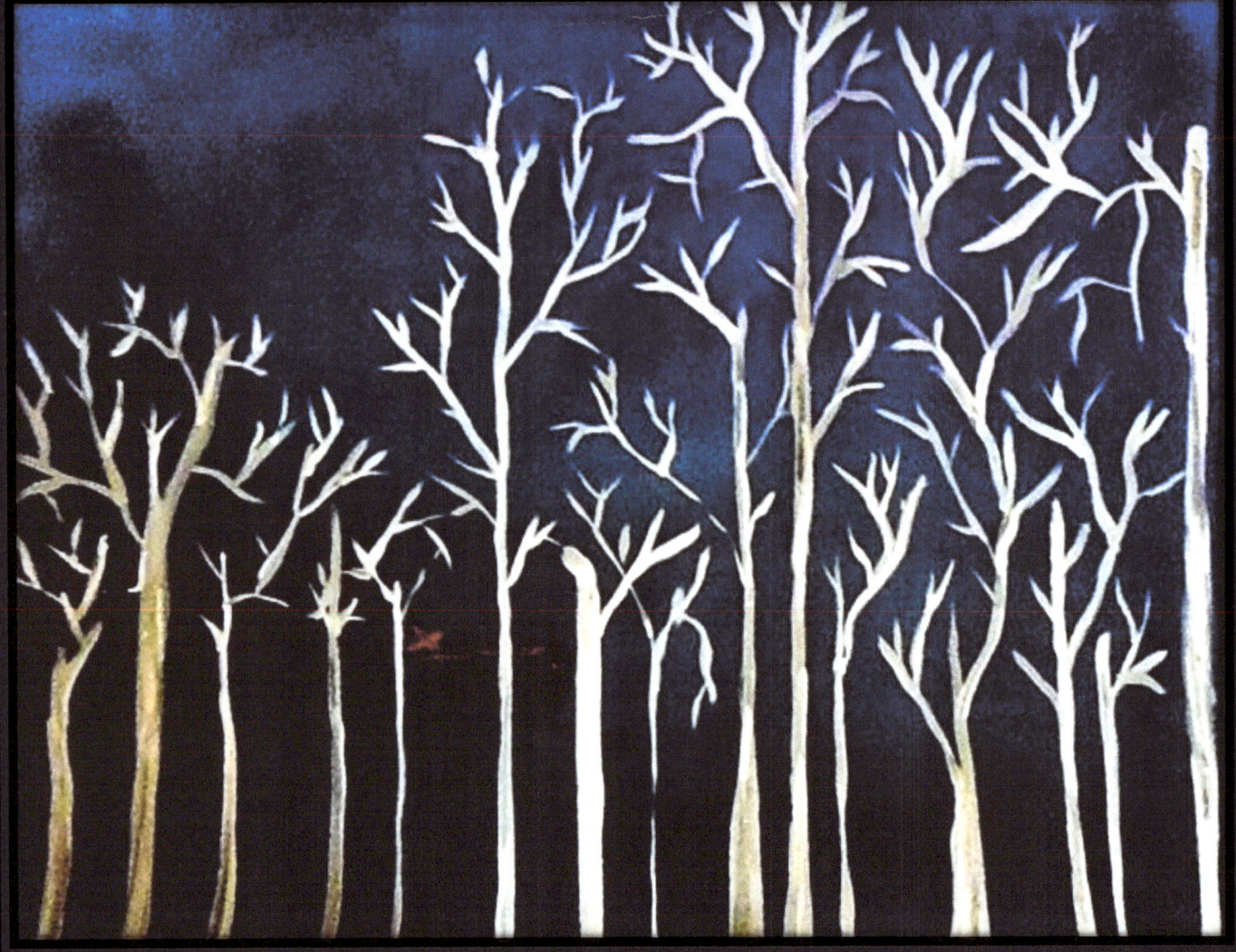

The Dream

Awoke from full breaths,
She knew.
The dream
That would bring
Dreams.
Closer to reality
Farther from destiny.

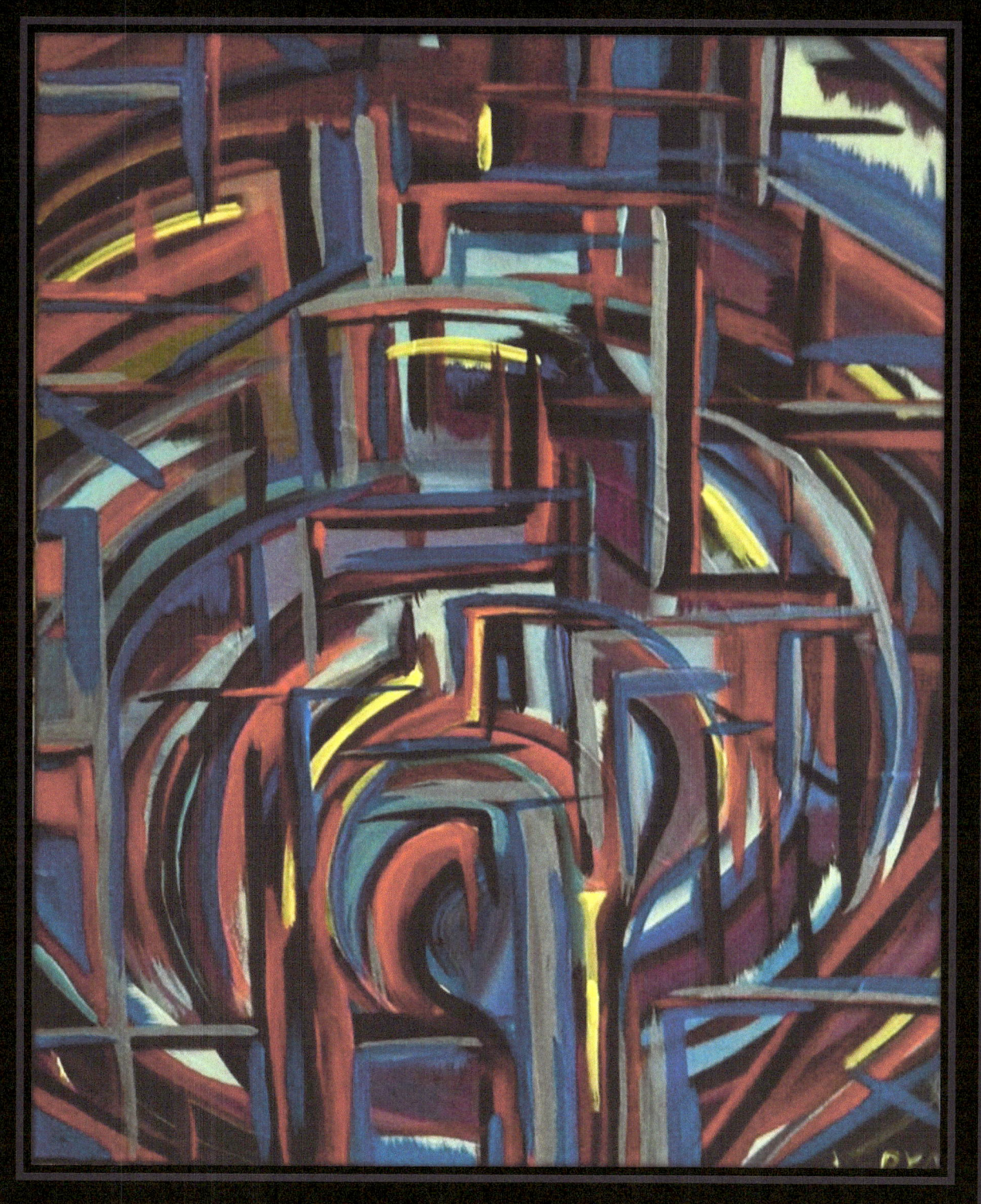

Divergent Convergence

In a twister
She searched for lines
Thinking she could hold on.
Lines turned into spheres
Lost again, she was.
Till she learned
The out.
Was,
in.

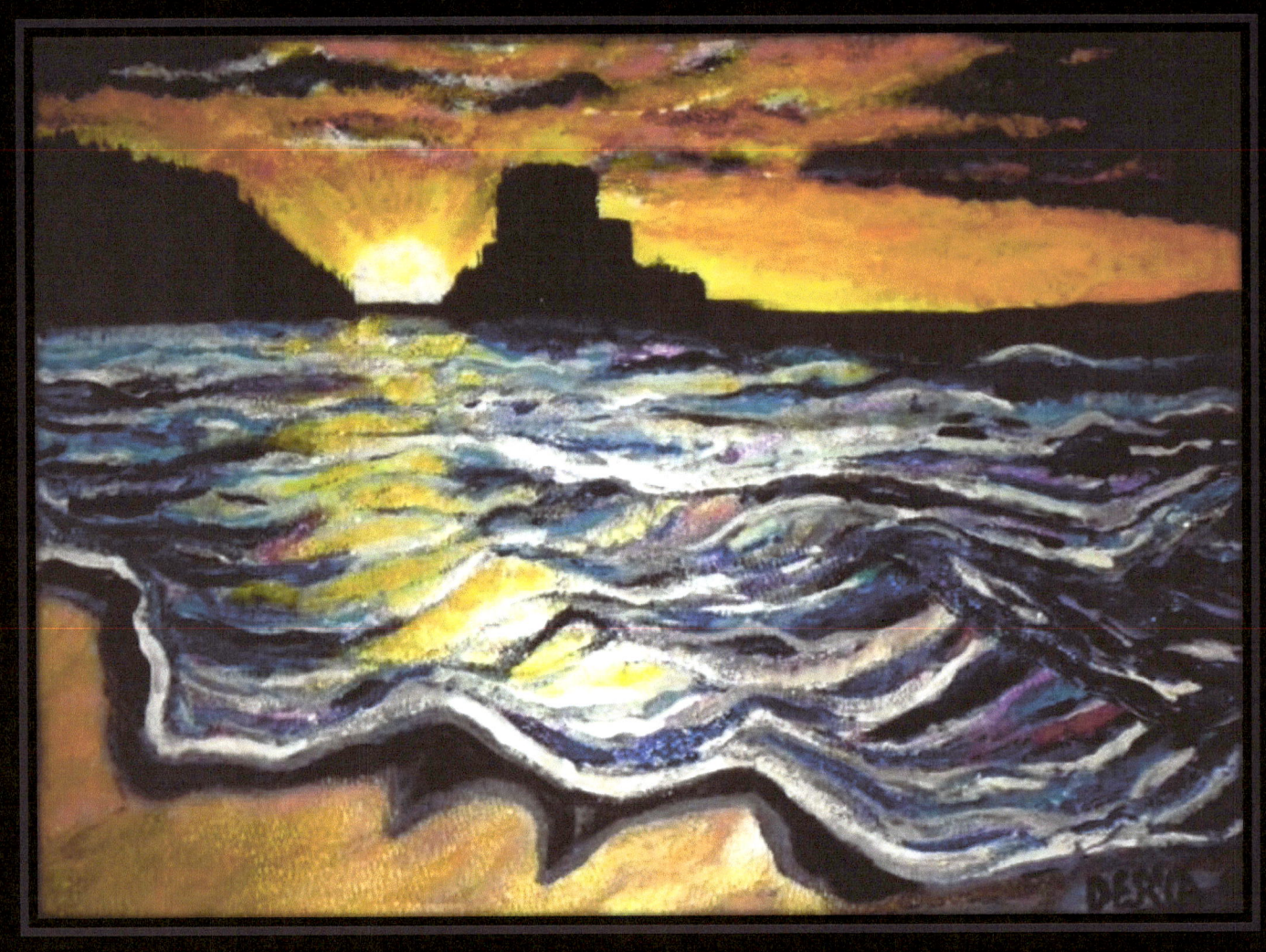

Water

A Saturday a.m.
Antalya. Turkey.
Like all Saturday's
On the same path.
She sat.
On the moist grains.
A whiff,
Salt, breeze, and algae.
Fresh.
Tickled her flesh.
Her long neck.
Stretched backwards.
Allowing.
She nodded and smiled
To waves, large and small.
It was the a.m.
That became her
Friend.

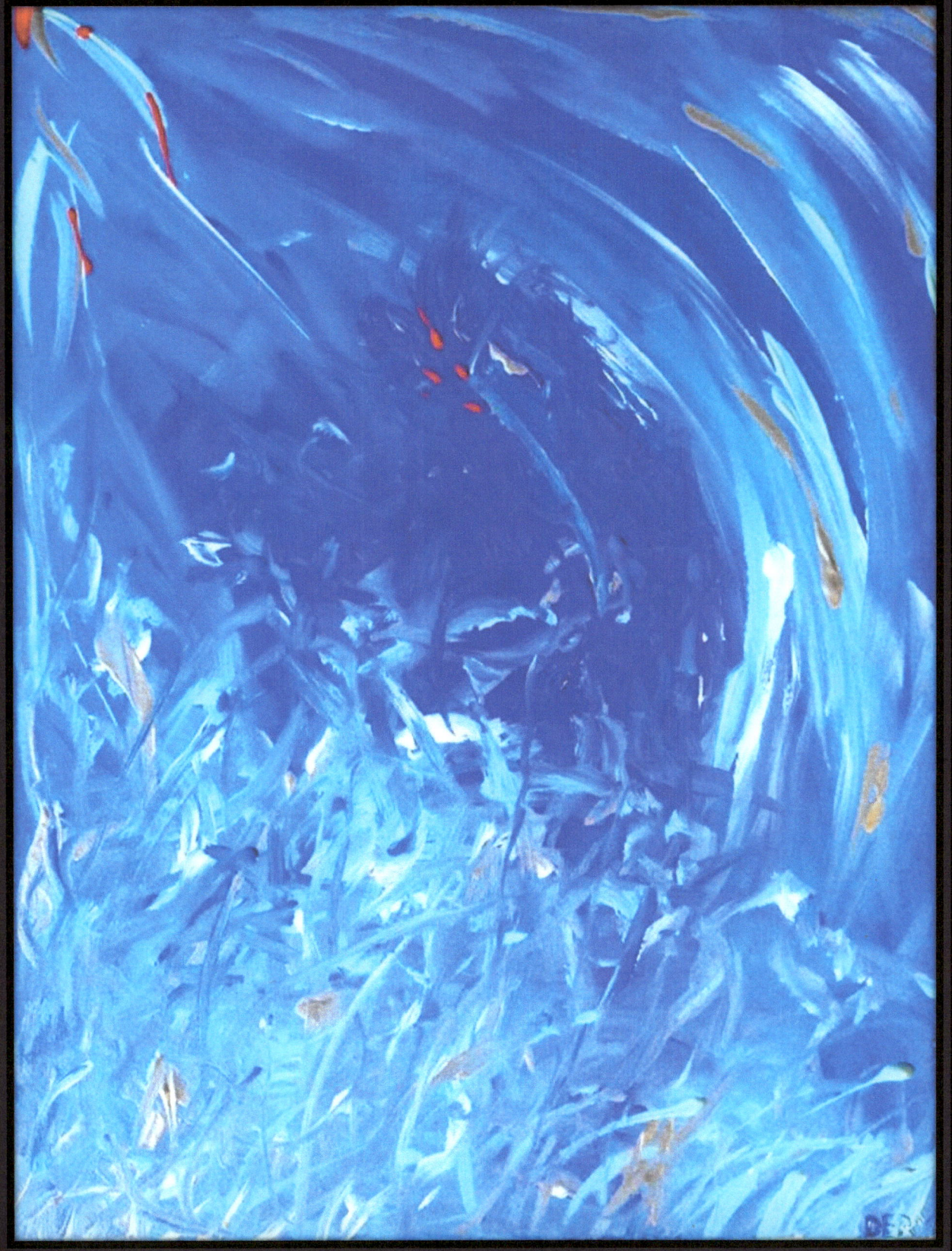

Zeal

A river flew through her
She knew
What was within.

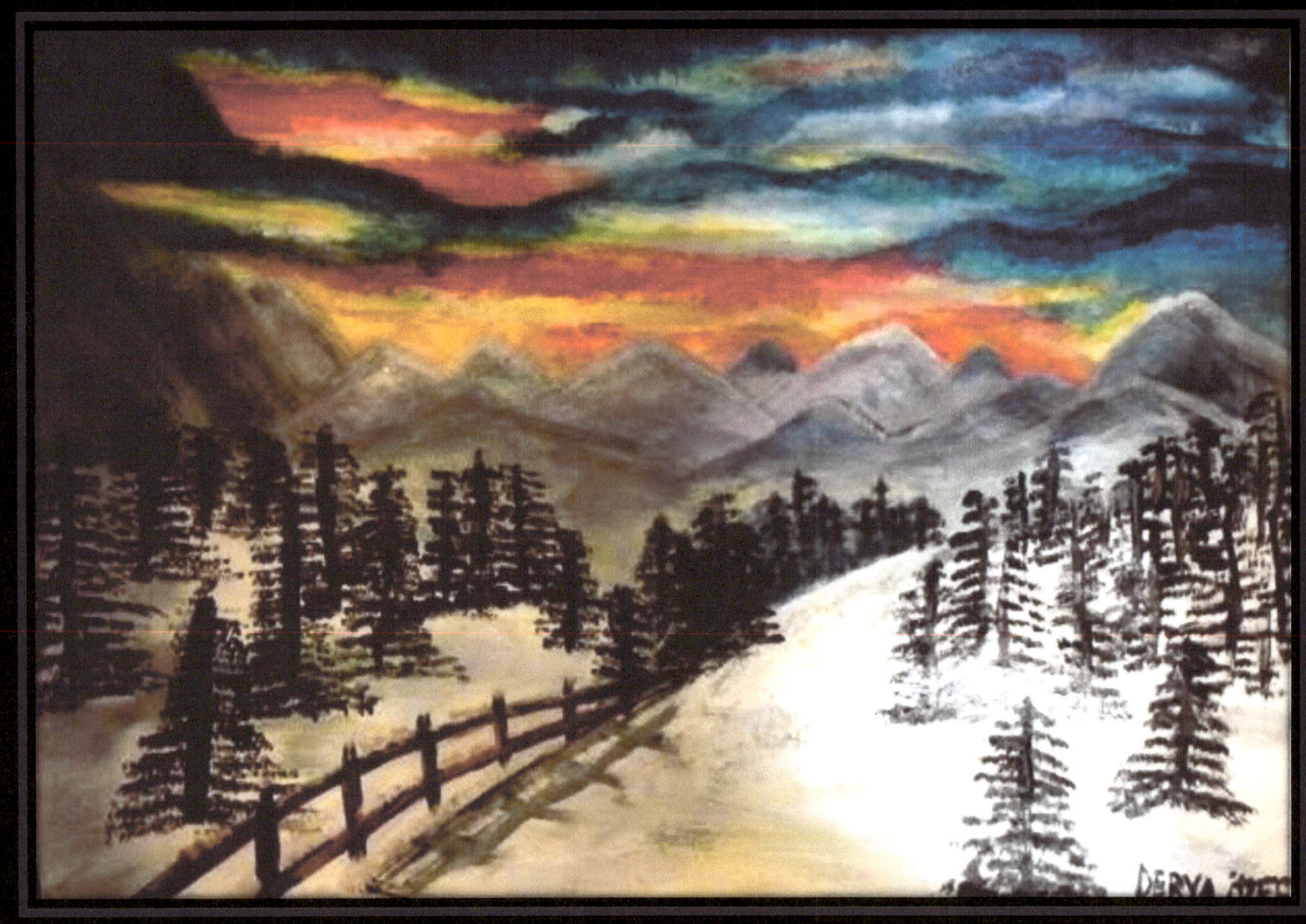

Clarity

It comes in waves
In the hues of the sky
It goes quick sometime.
Questioning
What is of permanence.
Like the mountains
Ahead,
They are there.
And then,
The mists of clouds.
They too appear.
Hoovering
The sky,
The trees,
The mountains,
You thought,
your vision was yours
and yet, that which you are
never is, still.

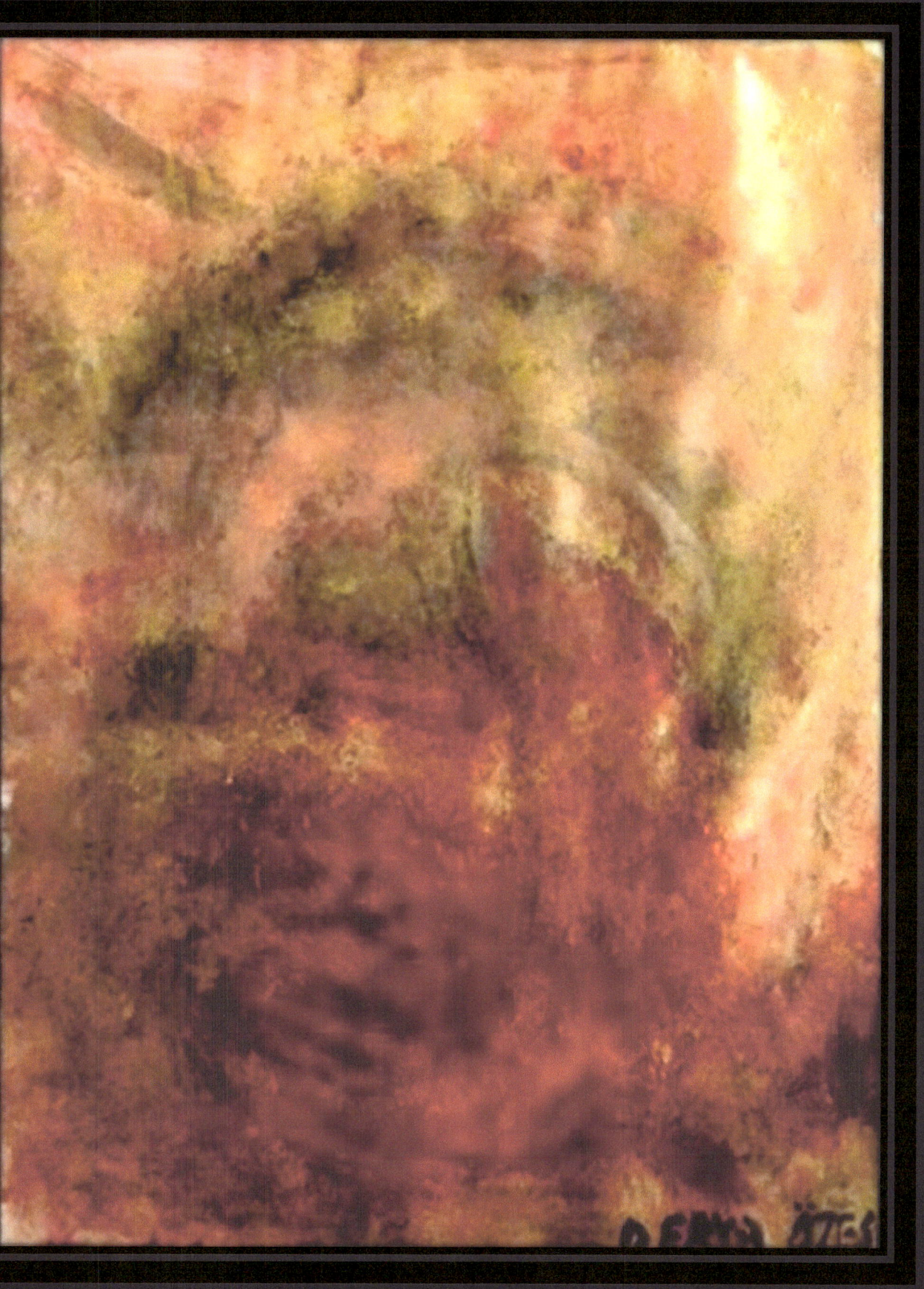

Chaos

We flutter with knots
With aimless joy
And pathless sorrow.

We flutter to the paradox
That which we are made of
And that which we give others.

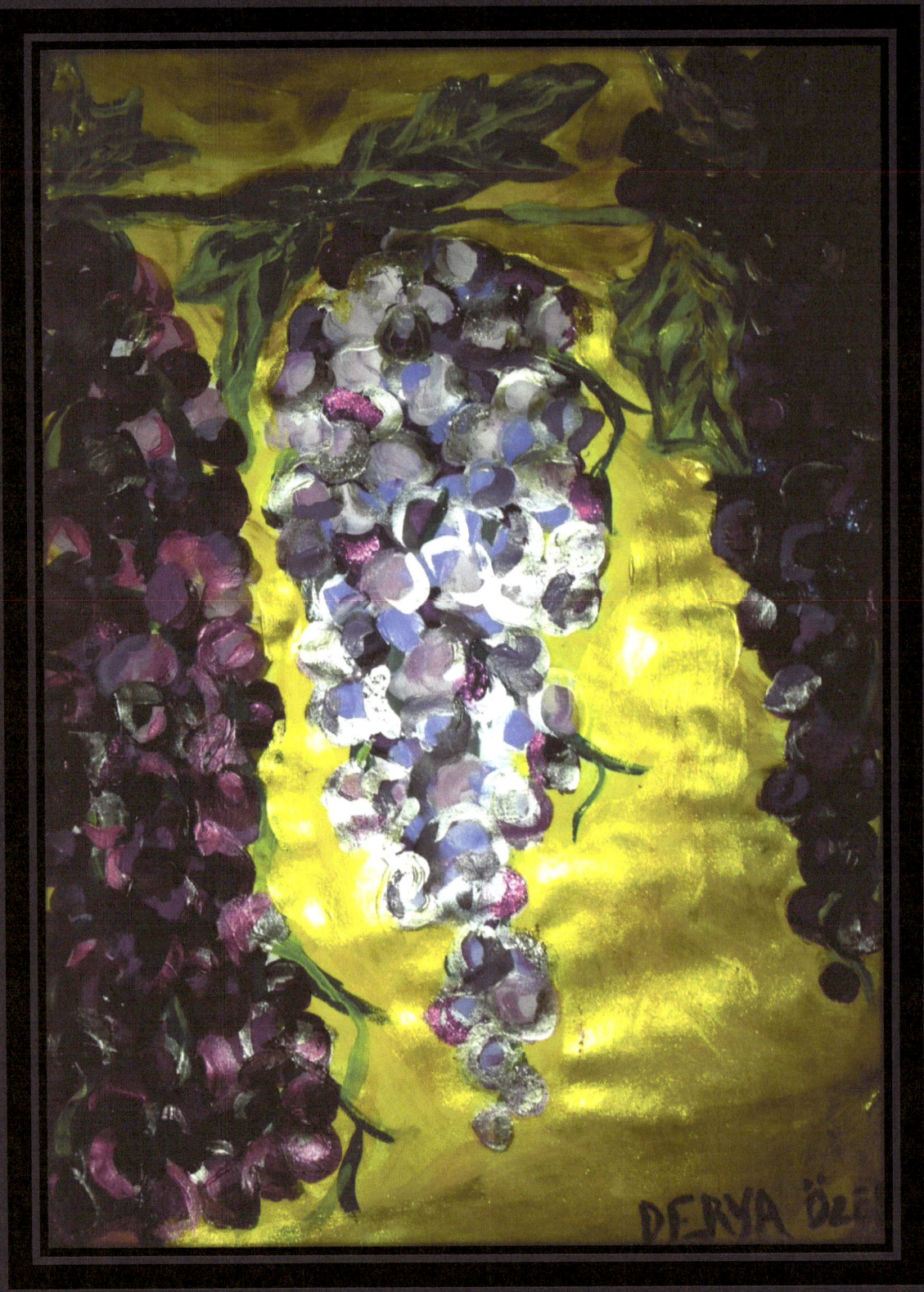

Bağ

My feet pressed,
in the sandy grains.
Touching the vines, plucking.
Some succulent. Some wizened.
they were,
of my grandmothers seed
and my mothers crop.

There I was, a foreigner
Yet, not.
I was visiting
And I wondered
what she thought of me
looking down
was I welcomed into her past?

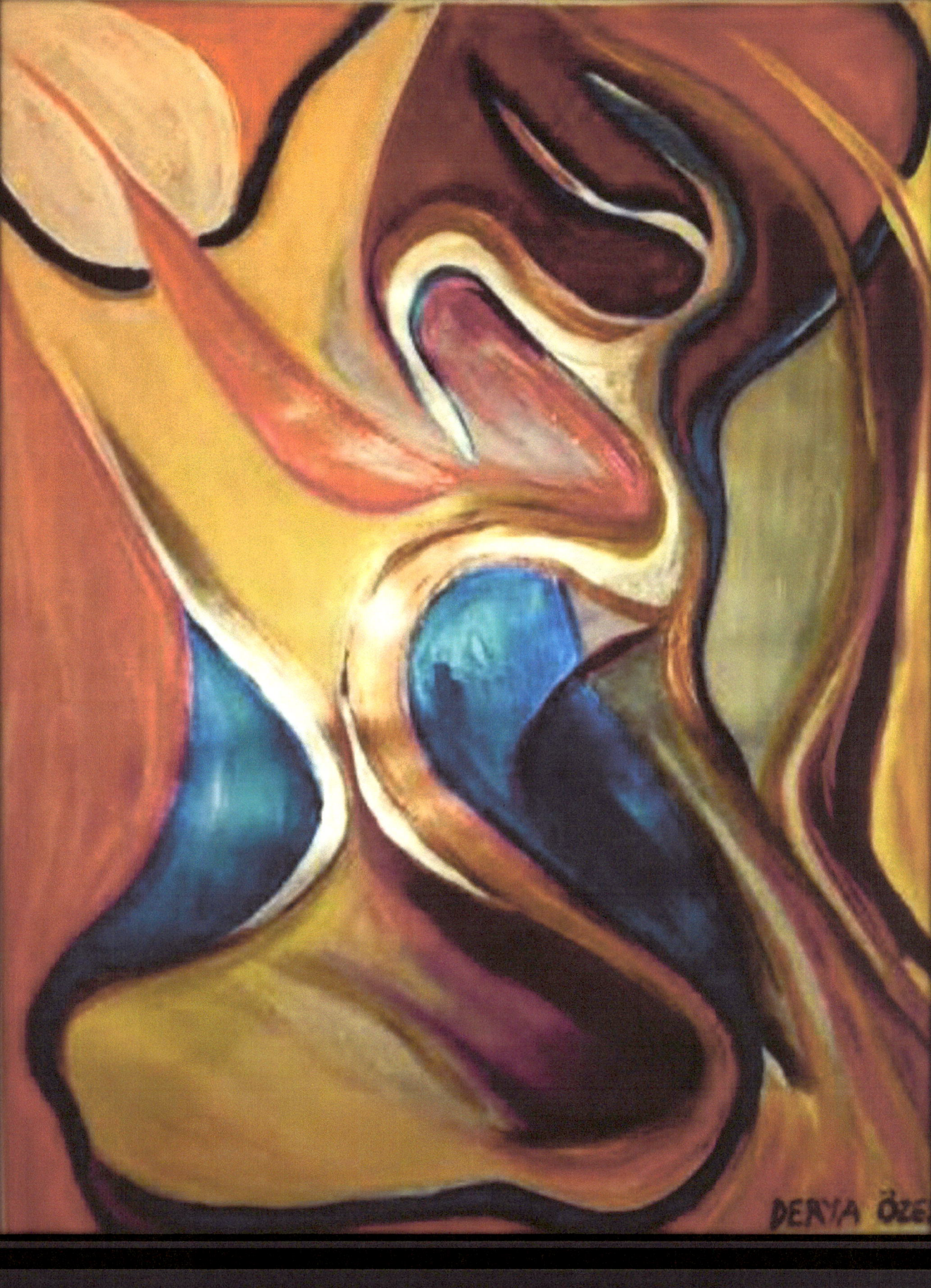

Ariossos

On an uninhabited mountain
far away
Alone
with the stars dancing above
like ferries
Feeling the dew

pressing from behind.
My hands grasp
the soil.
As warmth fills my heart
on a cold summer night
I whisper to God, I feel you.

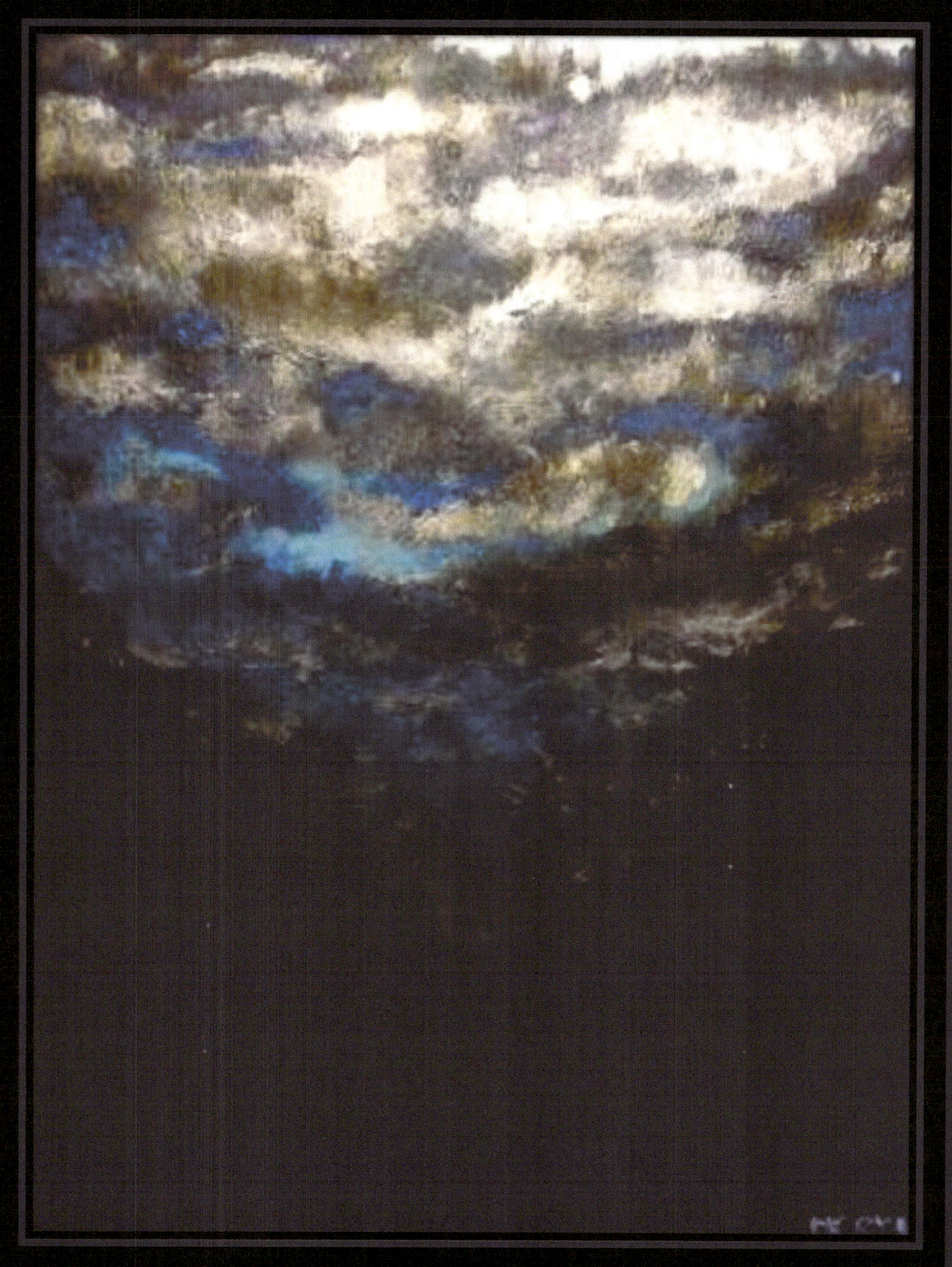

Omnipotent

It knows no silence
It speaks no words
It reminds all else, that they are not.

In

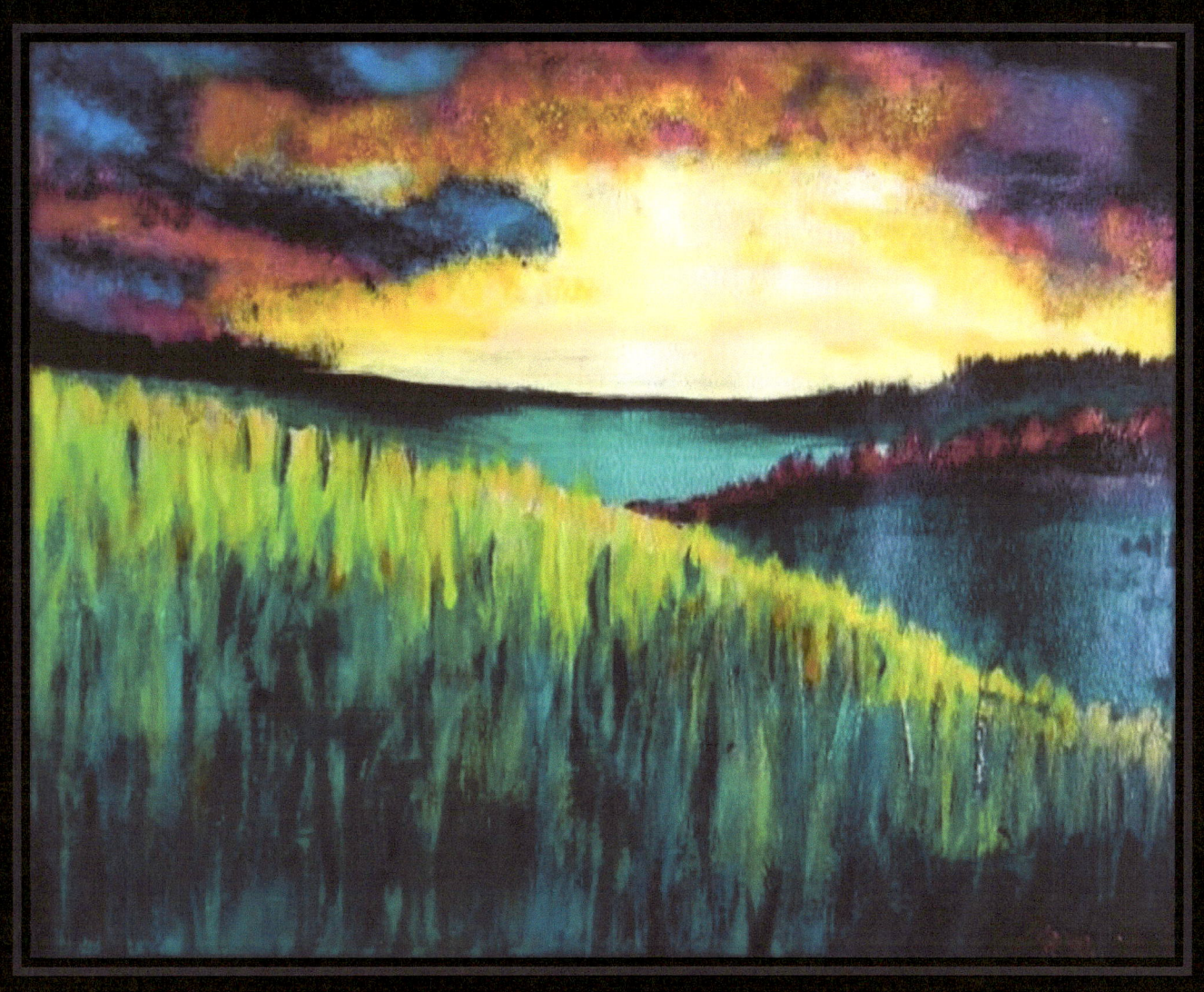

Echo's of my Grandmothers Past

My grandmother.
She lived in my mother's story.
Running within and around the wheat fields
She cropped every morning.
I imagined.
little mommy.
With mommy.
In the field,
Were daisy's.
She braided them
For my mother's cherish.
In the field
Lied the past
In the field,
Stories
for
the future.

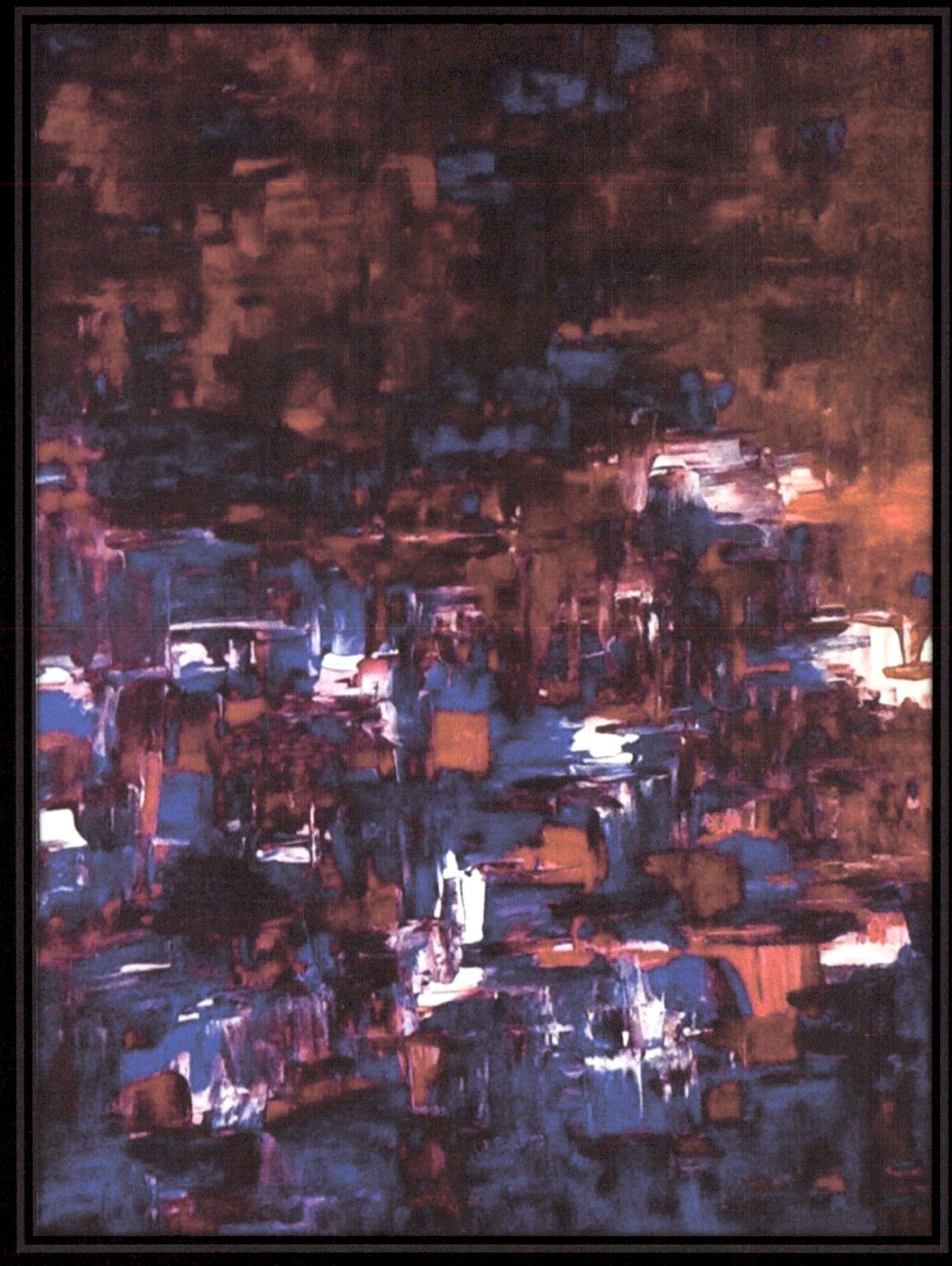

Dissonance

A current flows top to bottom
Sometimes creating splashes
Sometimes merging with the rocks ahead.
As it leaves trails and shadows
It becomes
Diamonds crest.

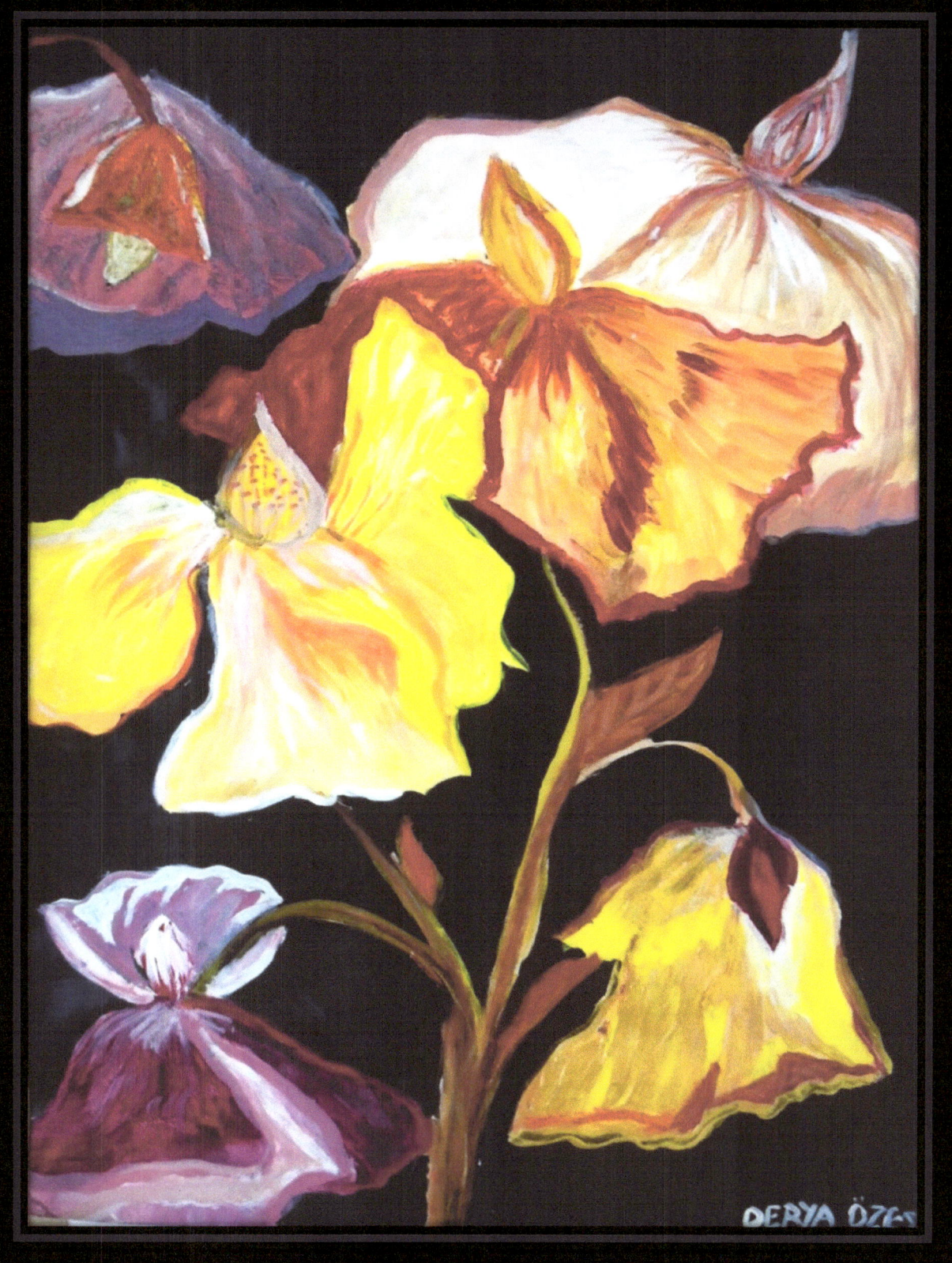

"Buruk "

In her pain,
She discovered many colors
The brightest stood tall.
The brightest bent low.
In her pain.
She discovered her cure.

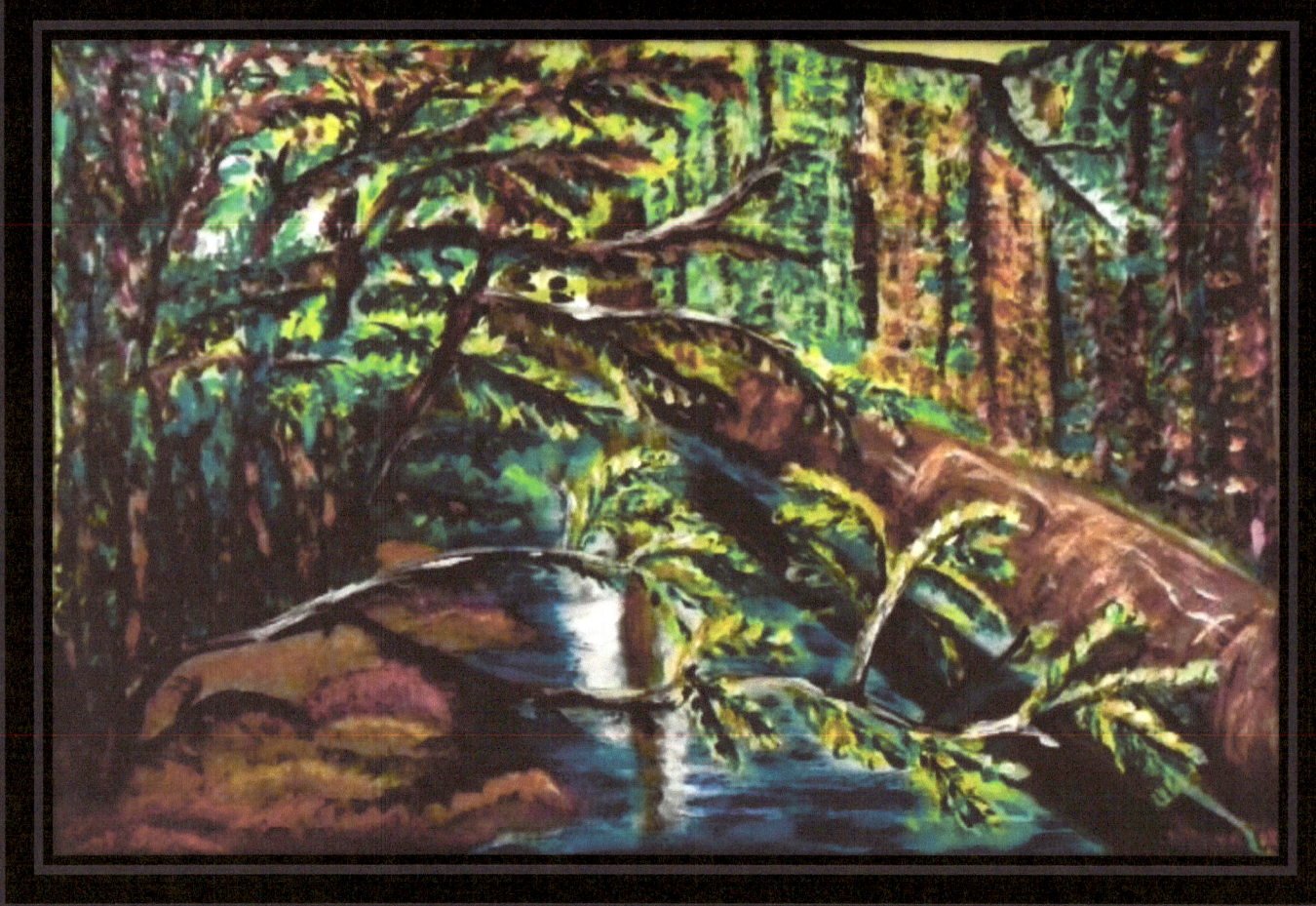

"Kader"

Nature does not question its meaning
It is birthed by the same source
We draw breaths from.
It smiles toward the sun.
It flows with the wind.
It remains naked in the rain
Bending when it has to,
Standing when it can.
Some of it falls apart.
Into the river
Into the soil.
To the wind
It goes,
If it has to.
It never asks why.
It turns red, green, and yellow.
But never black.
It is wise.
In its rawness.
It is elegant
In its humbleness.

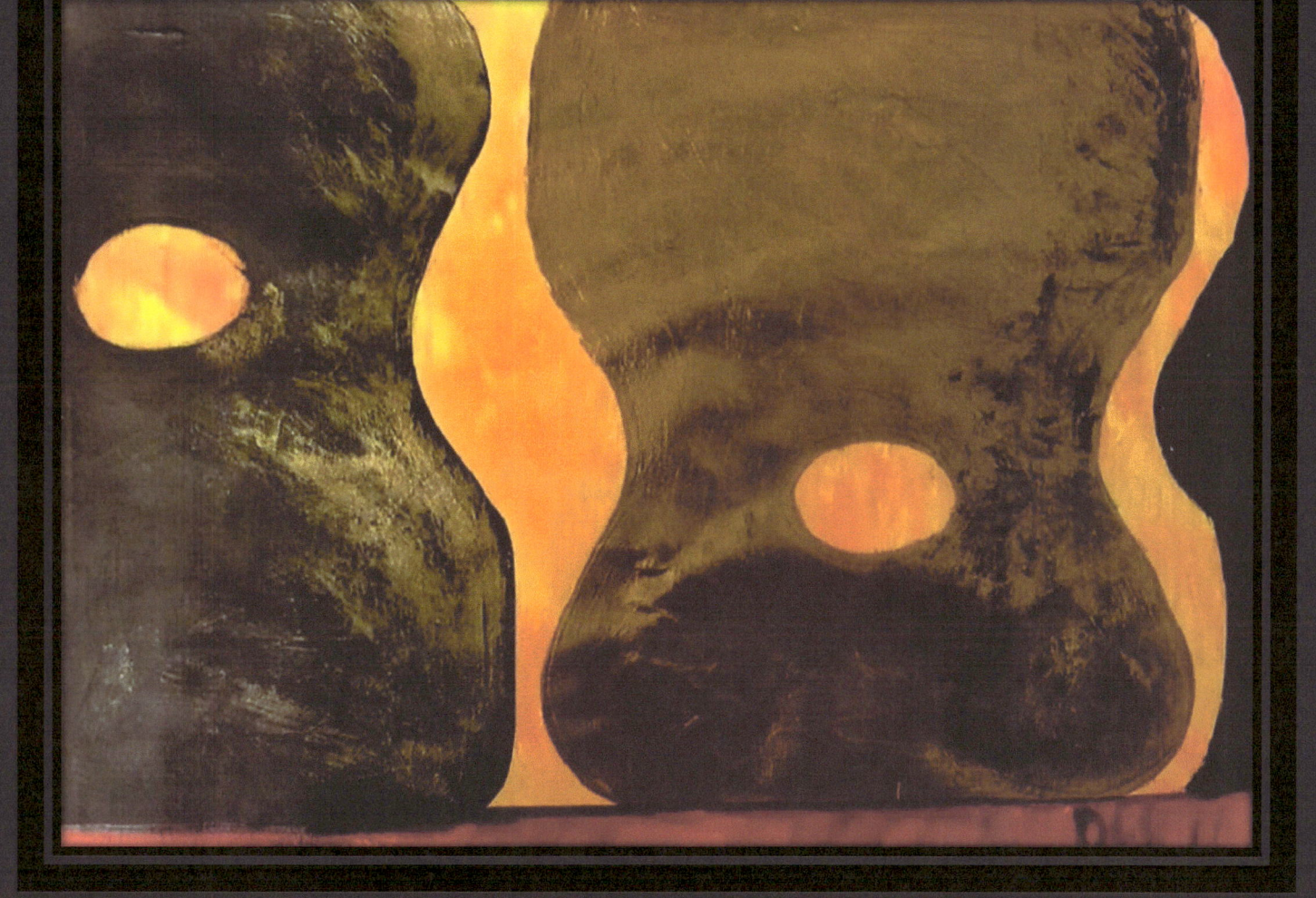

Contagious

No one can deny
How two
Resemble
One
We evolve
As we surrender.
We surrender
What we evolved.
None are
as they came.

Shadows

It was a warm summer evening
long hours of staring
Into the trickle
That dazzled
with the moon's shinning.
Her gaze followed the dancing.
Her feet allowed,

Slow and tiny steps,
On rocks big and small,
shadows casted everywhere.
All aimlessly there.
Pointing.
she knew,
Where to go then.

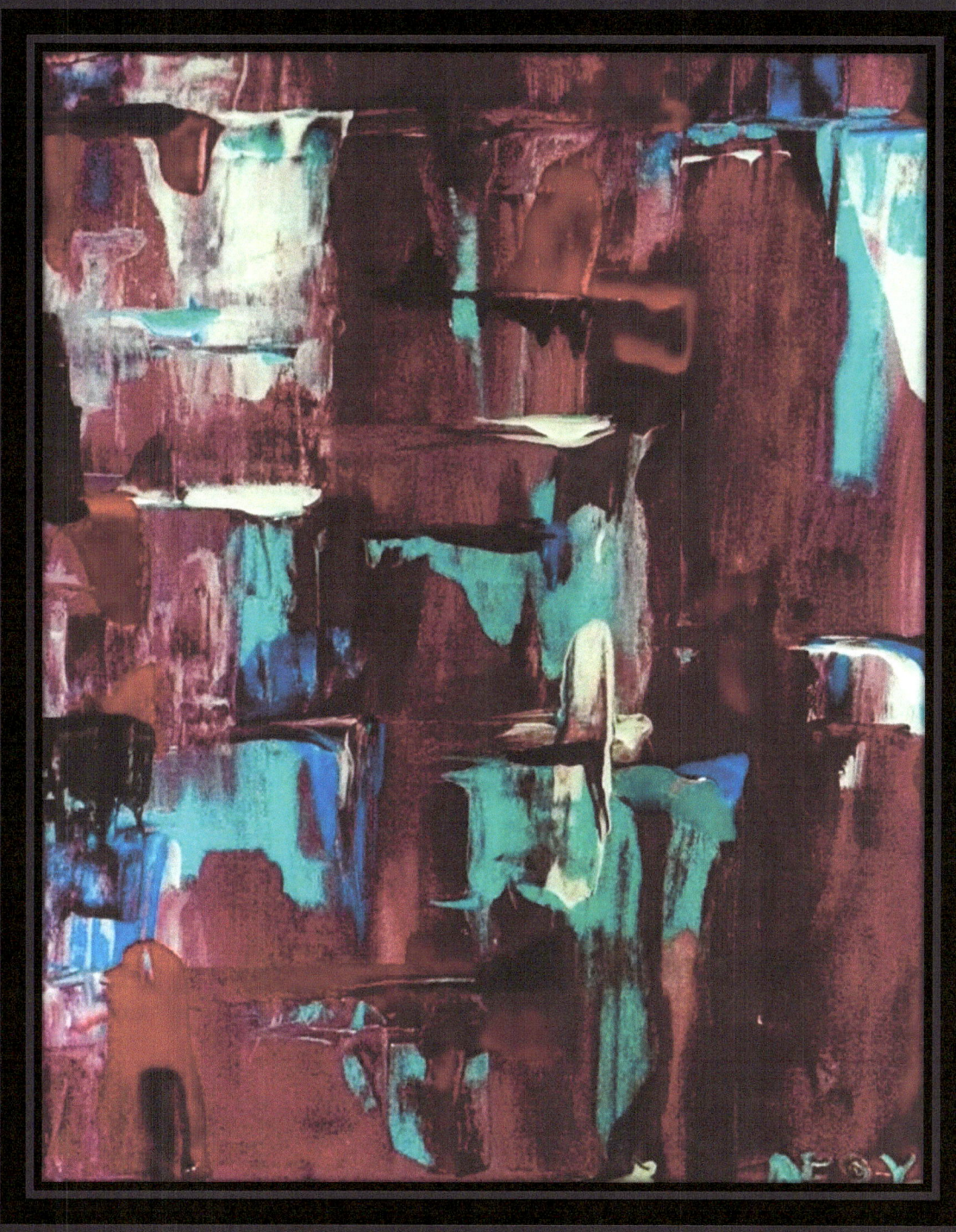

Hope

She was growing weary
Of time. Of words.
"It will be ok. It is worth it".
She knew this was so.
But she was human also.
The longing for the past.
The comfort she knew. She sought.
So vast it appeared
So close. Yet afar.

"It will be ok"
Was all she had.
It promised
A glow,
Within the darkness
So she believed
In the whispers of white and blue.
It will be ok.

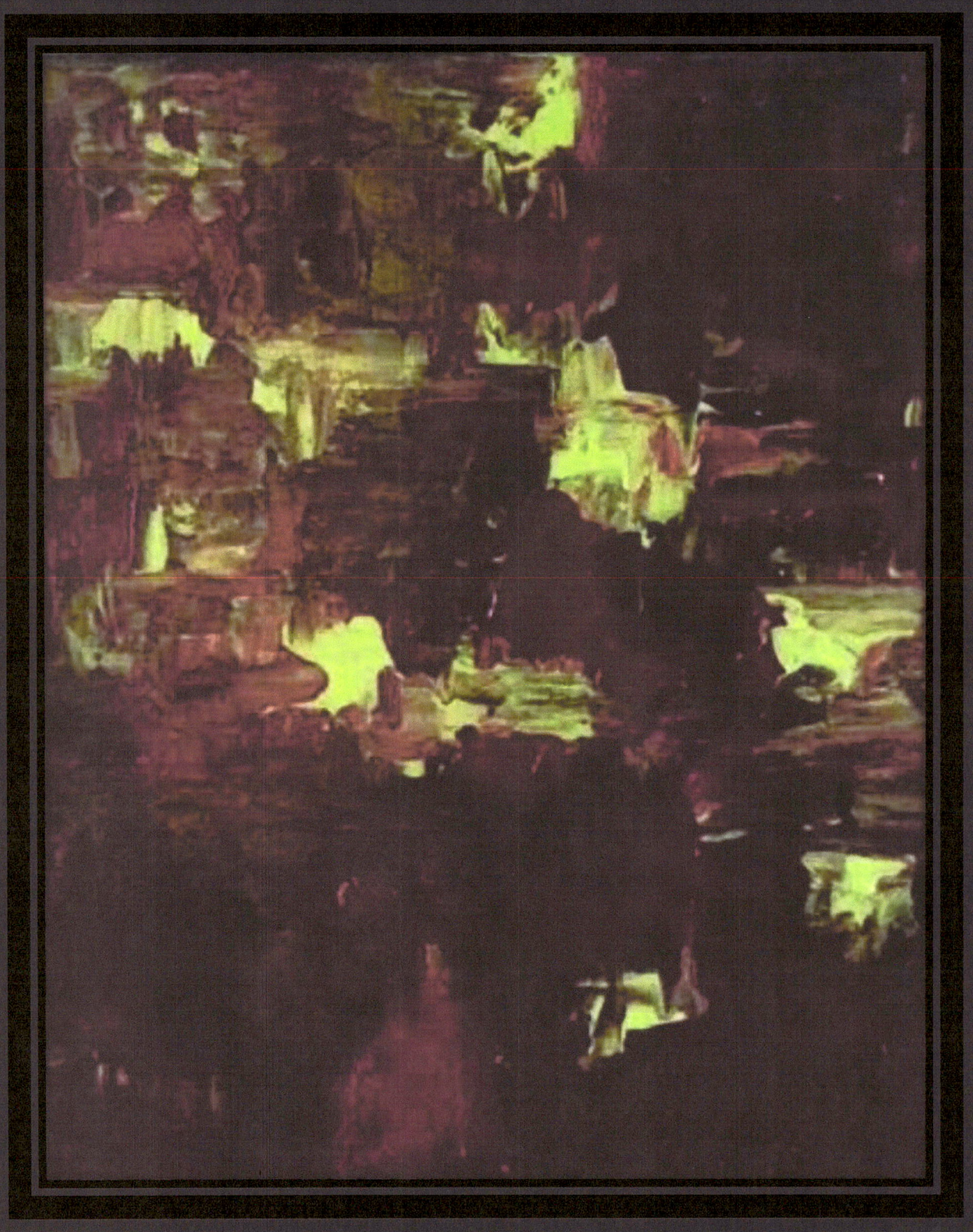

9

Odd enough to stand out
Even enough to be recognized
Nature is gold.
And red
Like the body's fold.

Yes.
An oddness within familiarity.
We are 9
We always were
We always will be.

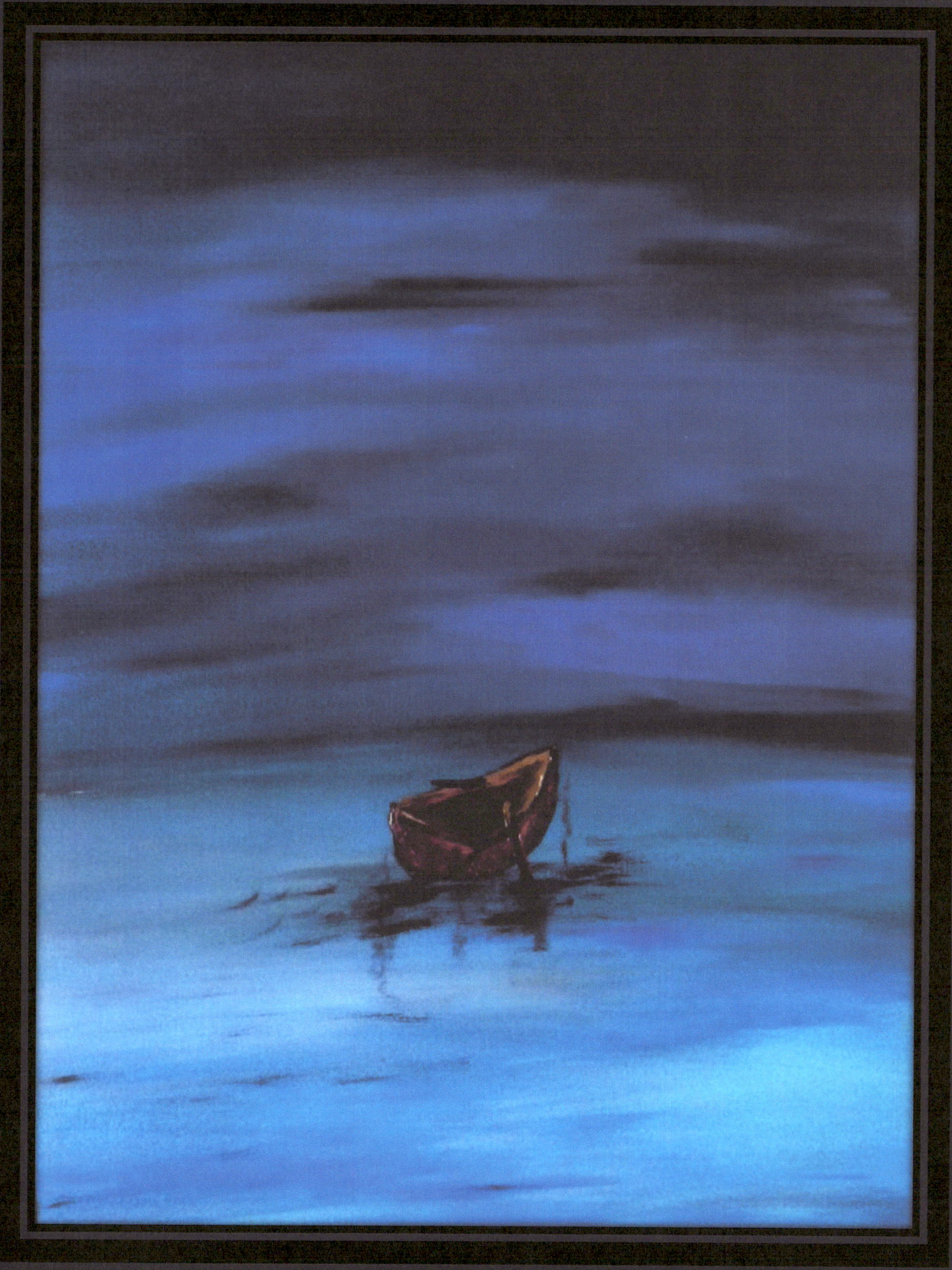

Forward

Toward a darkness,
She paddled.
For the sake of

Choice.
Freedom
Was her goal.

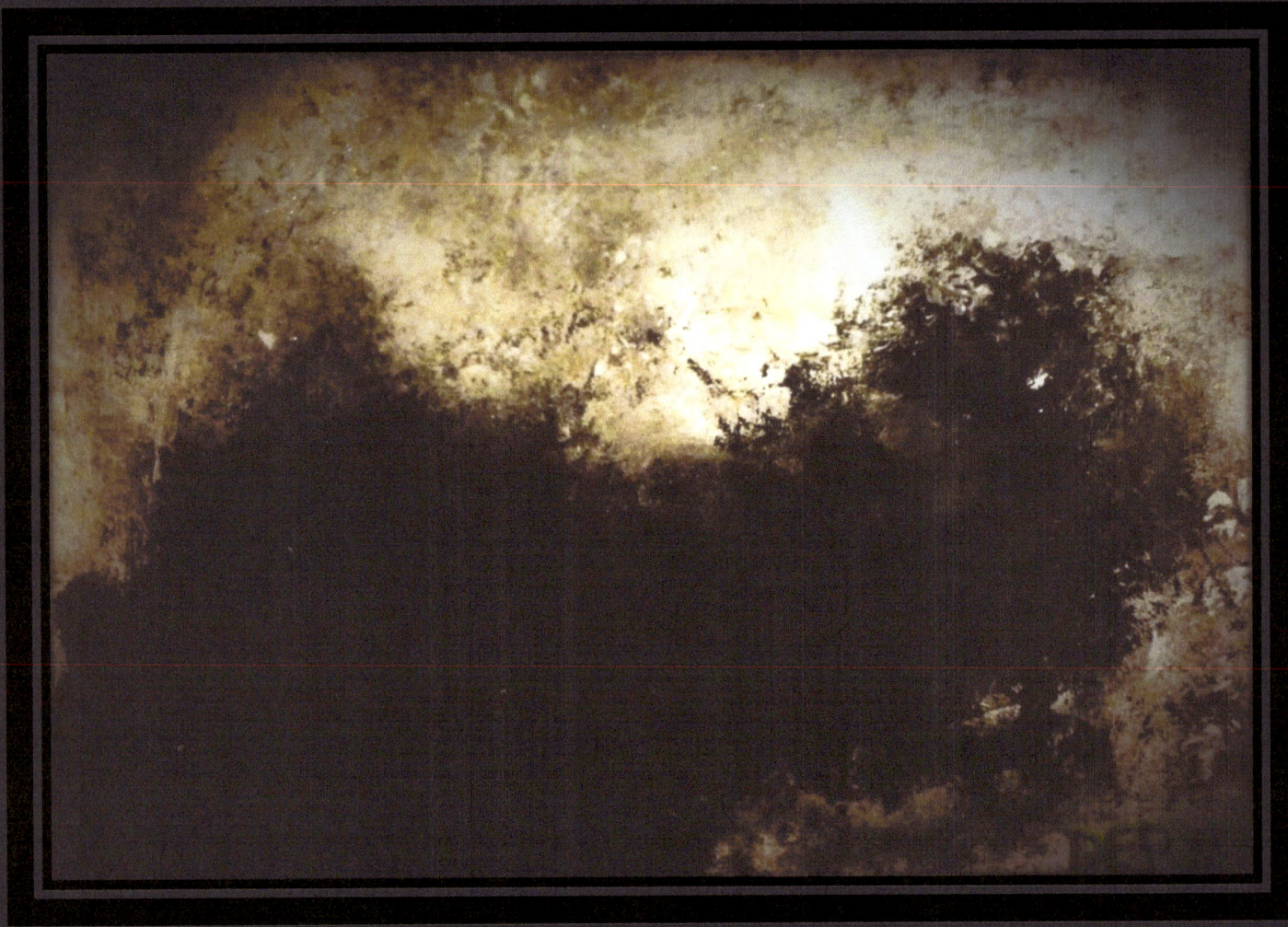

The Glimpse

Walking
11 pm strike.
Alone,
Cold.
Bundled,
Alone.
Walking
Focused.
Looking down.
Ahead,
Her path
Almost there.
Wanting

To be inside.
Call it over.
Enough she had.
Almost home.
Ten more steps.
She looked ahead
Her feet stopped.
Her eyes taken
Stayed put
Convinced herself
To go inside.
The day had.
Begun.

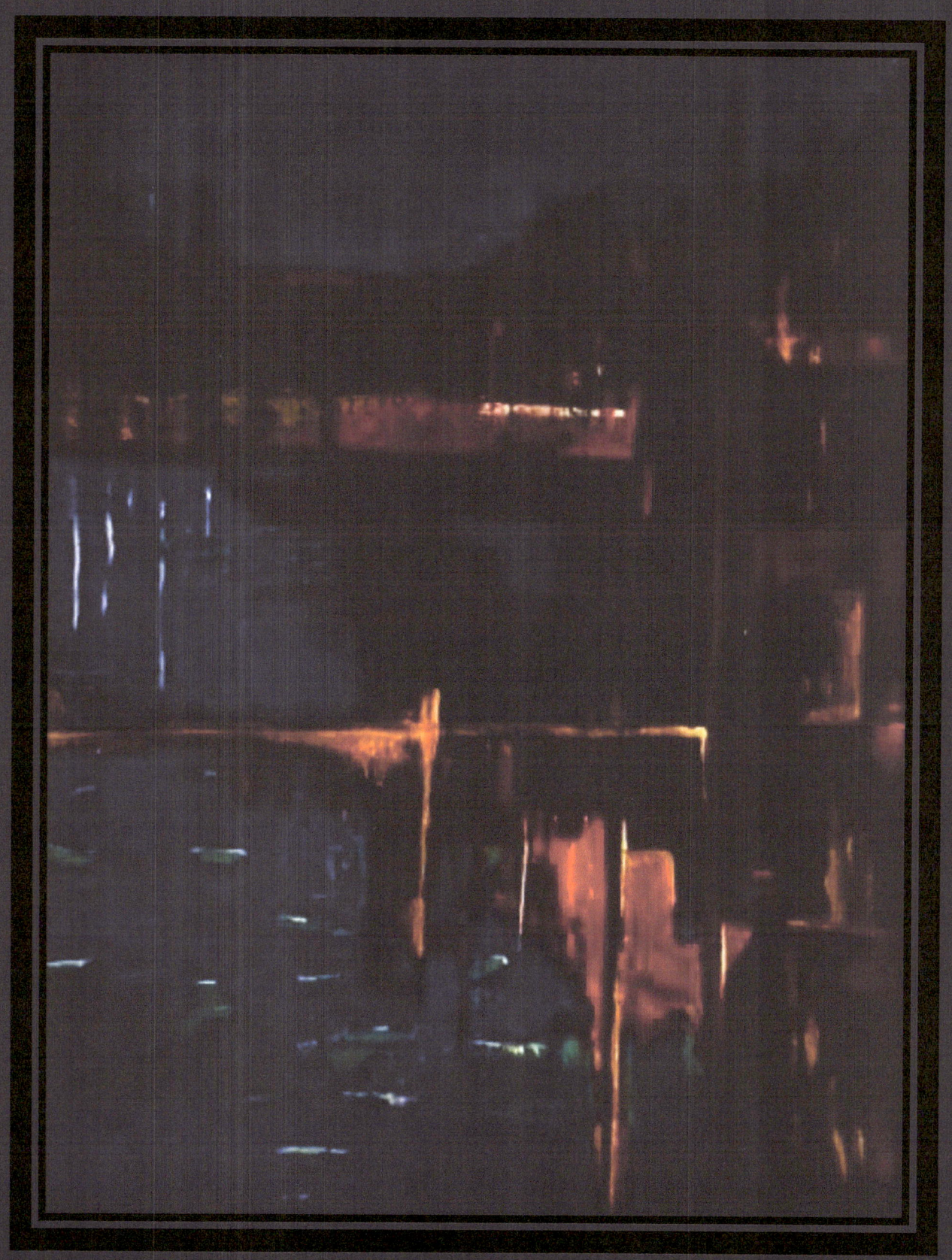

Open Doors

They were a story of the past

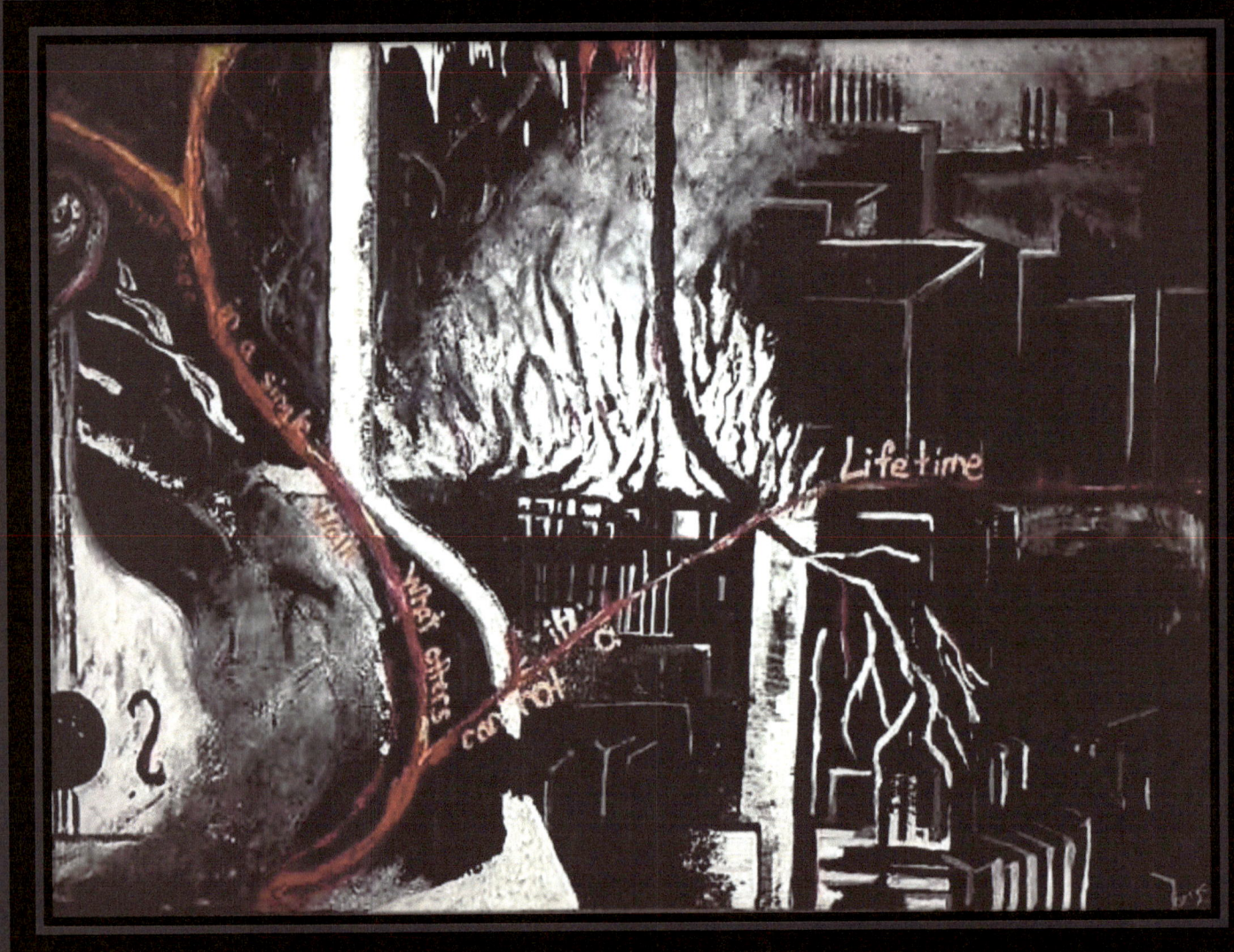

Insight

About the Artist

Derya is intrigued by how emotion, thought, language and knowing is revealed through one's self. She has a passion to notice and understand moments of insight. She finds painting to be a gateway to capturing higher forms of knowing.

Derya enjoys being with nature, listening to Turkish and Ottoman classical and folk music, playing the violin, taking professional photographs, reading and writing on topics pertaining to philosophy, psycho-linguistics, meta-cognition, and psychoanalysis.

To learn about Derya's professional endeavors, visit,
https://www.linkedin.com/in/deryaozes

To view updated paintings, visit,

www.deryart.org

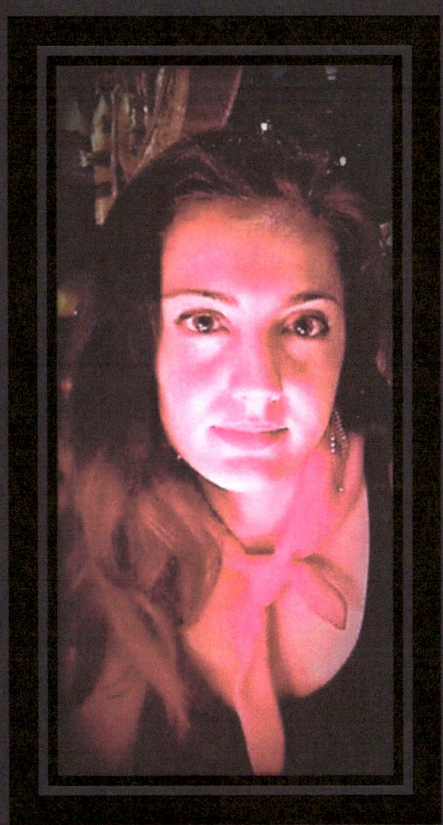

"As you live deeper in the heart, the mirror gets clearer and clear"- Rumi

This book can be purchased at,

www.createspace.com/6769660

www.amazon.com

and by, direct inquiry with the artist.

To inquire on availability of a painting, to purchase, or request a personalized painting, the artist can be contacted via,

deryaozturk9@gmail.com